Why Meditate to Enlightened Music?

It's kind of tricky to meditate in this age, and I've figured out a way to make it easy for you. It's to meditate to music. I have created a number of albums, which are designed to meditate to.

If you sit, if you make your mind quiet, if you're still and you listen to the music, the music will do two things.

The energy in the music is very high. I've gone into very high planes of consciousness, into samadhi, to bring a certain power into the music as a whole. And when you put on the [music], the energy is so high in it that it will simply block out the thoughts and impressions of the people in this world.

I have infused each of the albums with the light of enlightenment and with a tremendous amount of kundalini. I can't explain how it's done—but let's just say that it's hooked up to a certain dimensional access point.

When you listen to the songs, the level is actually there of a particular universe, a very high plane, and it will lift you up if you can just listen to it—into these higher dimensions—the same way it would if you were meditating with me or with another enlightened teacher.

When you put on the [music], essentially you're sitting down with an enlightened teacher and meditating with them.

—Rama, Chapter 1, "Meditation" (excerpts)

To access Rama's music for meditation, please visit
livingflow.com/music

The Enlightenment Cycle

TEACHINGS ON MEDITATION

AND ENLIGHTENMENT

"Spiritual knowledge is the experience of enlightenment and requires an understanding of the innermost workings of the **Enlightenment Cycle**," Master Fwap began.

"Spiritual knowledge is the awareness of the eternal side of things: the eternal side of ourselves, of others, and of the worlds that exist both within and outside of us."

"Enlightenment makes you happy!" Master Fwap responded with a broad smile. "It is the experience of ecstasy beyond anything you can possibly imagine. Knowledge of the **Enlightenment Cycle**—of the ways that the inner dimensions and nirvana work—gives you an entirely new perspective on everything. It lifts you far above the transient sorrows, pains, pleasures and joys that the unenlightened masses experience each and every day of their lives."

—from *Surfing the Himalayas*

Also By the Author

BOOKS
Surfing the Himalayas
Snowboarding to Nirvana
Insights: Tantric Buddhist
Reflections on Life

MUSIC
Enlightenment
Canyons of Light
Samadhi

The Enlightenment Cycle

TEACHINGS ON MEDITATION

AND ENLIGHTENMENT

Rama - Dr. Frederick Lenz

LIVING FLOW

Published 2002 by The Frederick P. Lenz Foundation for American Buddhism
Published 2016 by Mystic Buddha Publishing House

Published 2020 by Living Flow
www.livingflow.com
Boulder, CO 80302 USA

Paperback ISBN 978-1-947811-17-1
Ebook . . . ISBN 978-1-947811-18-8

Library of Congress Control Number: 2019952708

Publisher's Code r053-v38

Cover art & design by Meg Popovic
Interior dragon art by Janis Wilkins
Back cover photo by Greg Gorman

Preface

The Enlightenment Cycle series of talks is Rama – Dr. Frederick Lenz' introductory material for the new student of meditation and enlightenment. Rama explains how to meditate and specifically how to meditate in modern times, when we are living on a very crowded planet. He introduces his unique approach of combining traditional powerful methods of meditation with music that connects us directly to higher states of awareness.

Rama describes what enlightenment is and why it's worth seeking. He discusses fundamental and profound Buddhist and yogic concepts in a down-to-earth manner that's easy for people today in both the East and West to relate to. We learn about mindfulness, power, balance, wisdom, personal happiness, reincarnation, and the miraculous—directly from a modern day enlightened master.

This series of talks explains the core principles of practice with Rama's unique blend of clarity and humor. Since Rama was focused on updating Buddhist and yogic teachings for our era, he also describes how career can be used as part of the practice, especially technology and computer science careers.

After the release of the original *Enlightenment Cycle* talk series in 1992, Rama added two follow-on recordings: *Intermediate Meditation* and *The Enlightenment Cycle*. *Intermediate Meditation* provides additional instructions to the student who's been meditating daily for a few months or longer. Rama explains how additional focus techniques can be added to strengthen the meditative experience once the student has developed a basic practice.

The final talk, simply called *The Enlightenment Cycle*, provides a broad review and discussion of the pathway to enlightenment and why it's worth pursuing.

Each chapter in this book is a transcription of a recorded audio talk. The talks reflect the spontaneous tone that typified Rama's live seminars, which combined sophisticated descriptions of deep spiritual truths with warmth and humor, recalling stories of the Buddha and other enlightened teachers conversing with their students.

Rama's words will guide you on an entertaining and profound tour of meditation, magic, and enlightenment.

—The Editors

[To access Rama's music for meditation, please go to livingflow.com/music for more information.]

Contents

CHAPTER ONE

MEDITATION

Meditation is a process of expanding your awareness. When you meditate, you get in touch with the deepest part of yourself. You know from your own point of view what's right, what's wrong, what you should do and shouldn't in any situation. Meditation makes you tough, makes you strong, conscious, happy, and eventually, enlightened. Meditation is a process of silencing your thoughts.

Beyond the world of thought and sensorial impressions, there are planes and dimensions of perfect light, knowledge, and radiant perfection. Meditation is simply a process of moving your awareness field from the awareness of this world, from the awareness of time and space, into eternity, into the eternal dimensions.

The world you see around you is largely physical. It's perceived through seeing, tasting, smelling, touching and feeling. It's also analyzed through thought, it's felt through emotion, it's remembered through memory, anticipated through projection, and experienced as now. But there are different modes and levels of perception, which most people are not familiar with. And there are different universes, astral universes, and above the astral universes, the planes of light and beyond the planes of light, nirvana itself—perfect enlightenment, the essence and nexus of all things.

Meditation is about becoming conscious of who you are, becoming happy, relaxing, slowing down, and chilling out and learning to smile. It's also about very profound things that are hard to express in words—about beauty, just about being most excellent at everything, finding the perfect part of yourself, overcoming your self-destructive tendencies, overcoming depression, anxiety, nervousness, fears of all types and descriptions. It's about being happy, being conscious, being free, and most of all about being who you really are, which is something that most people don't have any consistent consciousness of.

Meditation is eternal awareness. The height of meditation is normally symbolized by the Buddha, a person who yokes their mind—through the practice of yoga, meditation, Buddhism—with the highest light in the universe. They experience it in a state called *samadhi*. Samadhi is a complete cosmic consciousness experience. It's like climbing to the top of the Himalayas and just seeing the ranges, the mountains up there—an experience that really is unparalleled. It just can't be expressed in words. Meditation is a journey, a journey to the other side. The other side can't be explained—the mystical worlds, the timeless, miraculous worlds of light. But they can be certainly, most certainly, experienced by you.

So this tape is about how to meditate.

Meditation is essentially a wonderfully easy process ... unless you live in this age, in which case it's hard. Oh, maybe it's hard. Meditation is about making your mind calm and quiet, and if the earth was not overpopulated and toxic, this is a very easy thing to do. The mind is not naturally so active. But there are two factors you have to take into consideration—a crowded planet and the fact that we're all psychic.

Each human being has an aura. An aura is the energy body that surrounds your physical body. And your body of energy gives off impressions just like radio waves—short wave, long wave—and you feel those impressions. You feel the thoughts, the feelings of others, particularly people, of course, you're in close contact with, either physically or emotionally. You're very open to them. But you also feel the vibrations of the people in your neighborhood, at your school, where you work, where you drive your car, your town, your state, your country and your planet. But most particularly you feel the vibrations in a radius of about 100 miles from where your physical body is.

Everyone is psychic. People just don't know that. They think so much; they worry so much. They're so caught up in unhappy emotions. They're not still enough. They're not wise and silent enough to see that 90 percent of what they think and feel is alien to them. Ninety percent of what they think and feel—90 percent of what *you* think and feel—are not your own thoughts and emotions. They're somebody else's—a lot of other people's.

I always remember an adventure of "Star Trek" where Spock is explaining to Captain Kirk that people come to Vulcan from other planets not so much to learn to be psychic, but people who come with psychic abilities learn to block out psychic impressions. That's what the advanced psychics teach them. At Vulcan, they teach them how to keep other people's thoughts out of their minds. And Kirk thought they went there, of course, to learn to be psychic. That's not the problem. Everyone's psychic. The difficulty is just having your own thoughts and feelings. Because if you don't, you can't possibly know who you are, what you care about; and you end up doing things, thinking things, wanting things, fearing things, that have nothing to do with you. They're somebody else's ideas, thoughts and feelings. It's absurd. But everybody does it.

Meditation is a process of not doing that. It's a process of not doing. It's about being still, being centered, being clear, being happy, being organically in touch with the universal light, developing parts of yourself that are unknown to most people, very powerful parts, very beautiful parts, very strong parts.

The billions of people on this overcrowded planet put out so much energy and so much of it is unhappy, that it makes everybody's minds active.

Everybody is thinking all the time, stressed out, can't slow down, can't feel what lies beyond this dimension. Normally it's very easy to do that. If you don't believe me, take a walk in the woods. Find a nice wooded path that not too many people have been on, where there are not a lot of impressions. Take a walk. Take a hike. And you will notice that your mind, if you monitor it, it becomes very quiet. You don't think much.

Now let's leave there and go out and walk down a city street. Drive on a highway and walk through a building. If you begin to examine your thoughts, you will observe that they change from where you are to the next locale. In other words, they're influenced. Go into a room with unhappy people, you'll find you get depressed, pulled down by their energy. Go into a place with happy people and you'll find you are brought up.

If we lived on a planet in which everyone was happy and progressive and it wasn't so overcrowded—getting more so every day—it would be very easy to meditate, very easy to feel infinity, to be in tune with our spiritual self. But that's not the case. And when you meditate, in particular, and you slow your thoughts down, you actually become more sensitive. You become more psychic because you are clearing yourself of thoughts and impressions of this world so you can feel the other world. You can feel the perfect worlds of light that exist beyond this plane.

It's kind of tricky to meditate in this age, in short, and I've figured out a way to do it, to make it easy for you. It's to meditate to music. I have created a number of albums, two in particular, which are designed to meditate to. There's one for morning meditation and one for evening meditation. There are 15 songs on each album. They're about four minutes each. And each album is designed to provide a morning or an evening meditation. The *Enlightenment* tape is for morning meditation. *Canyons of Light* is for evening meditation.

To meditate, all you need to do is sit down, either in a cross-legged position on a rug or outside on the grass or some place that feels good to you, or sit in a chair. Your back needs to be straight, though. Don't lie down. When you lie down, it's almost impossible to meditate because your body relaxes too much and you just kind of get sleepy. It's best to be very alert when you meditate. It's a nice idea to wash your hands and face, or, if it's a morning meditation, maybe to get up and take a shower, have a cup of tea or coffee or whatever wakes you up.

Sit down, relax, and if it's a morning meditation, put on the *Enlightenment* tape.

Each of the 15 songs has been composed around a dimension, and they're in ascending order. The morning tape offers you an experience of 15 different higher dimensions of light that provide the energy, the insight and the power to go out and have a wonderful day.

The evening meditation tape, *Canyons of Light,* references 15 other dimensions that are easier to get into at night, and you'll go very high in them. It's easier to meditate at night because in the evening people shut down. They get kind of quiet. They go home, fall asleep. And the dimensions that are available—some are easy to get to at night, some in the morning. The *Enlightenment* album is an hour long. If you are new to meditation, you might just want to meditate for half that time until you get your pace and your stamina built up, and then do the hour. The hour is great.

You might sit down in the morning, put on the tape and listen. Zazen, which is the name of our music group composed of myself and three other students of mine. Zazen is a Japanese word. It means to sit in silence, to listen, to be aware of everything and nothing and what's beyond both. Zazen is also a sitting meditation in Zen Buddhism.

If you sit, if you make your mind quiet, if you're still and you listen to the music, the music will do two things. One, it will provide a kind of an auric blanket. The energy in the music is very high. I've gone into very high planes of consciousness, into samadhi, to bring a certain power into the music as a whole. And when you put on the tape, the energy is so high in it that it will simply block out the thoughts and impressions of the people in this world so you will just be … safe. It's as if you're sitting in a pristine environment, in a beautiful power spot with no impressions. And it's very easy to touch the other worlds. But, secondly, all the songs are in groups of five. In other words, there are three groups of five on the first and three groups of five on the second albums. And the songs reference particular chakras.

A word about *chakras,* energy centers, and the subtle body and the doorways to infinity. There are three primary meridians in the body. There is a body of light, also known as the subtle body or the astral body, that surrounds your physical body. It is composed of a network of filaments or fibers of light, and those fibers join at places that we call chakras. There are seven primary chakras, and they run from the base of the spine to the top of the head. They are connected by three astral nerve tubes, the largest of which is the *shushumna,* and then there is the *ida* and the *pingala.*

The base chakra, the root chakra, which is where the *kundalini* energy is at rest, is at the base of the spine. Around the area of the sex organs there is a second chakra. The third chakra is around the navel area and a little bit below—about an inch below the navel.

Chakras are not in the physical body, but they correspond to these spots. They're in your energy body. The three lower chakras are the power chakras, and when you start to meditate, you should meditate first on the navel center. By meditating on your navel center you'll bring up the *chi,* the kundalini, from the lower centers. It'll come up from the lower two centers, and it's very easy to enter the navel center and bring the power up to that spot.

For the first five songs in the morning or evening tape, meditate on your navel center. Simply hold your attention—feel the area around your navel, about an inch below. If you have never done this before, if you are new to this process, simply place your fingertips of the right or left hand about an inch below your navel and press very gently.

Now close your eyes and feel the spot. The first few times you meditate like this, you can keep your fingers there if it helps you. It's not necessary to really visualize anything. You don't have to hold a picture in your mind. Simply feel the spot. As you become adept at meditation, you'll have no trouble feeling the spot because there will be tremendously beautiful surges of energy, of kundalini energy, around that chakra. But in the beginning, sometimes it's helpful just to put the fingers there—very gently.

Hold your attention on the navel area and listen to the five songs. Each of the songs is very different—the first five—and they are designed in an ascending order. They reference different planes of light, and you move from one to another—you climb up the ladder of light just by listening to them. Then, when those five songs have ended, move your attention to the center of your chest.

The next chakra up is called the heart chakra. It's in the center of the chest. If you hold your attention there—same thing. If you want to, you can put your fingers there and apply a little pressure. Hold your attention on the center of your chest, gently press very lightly and listen to the next five songs.

The chest center, the heart chakra, and the chakra above it—the throat center at the base of the throat—are the centers of balance, of happiness. The best chakra, the easiest to activate, is the heart center, and it will also pick up the throat center for you. If you hold your attention there for five songs, you'll feel tremendous happiness, brightness. You might see vivid colors. You might feel sensations of lightness. But if you just listen deeply, you'll stop thought. The same thing will happen with your navel center and with the third eye.

After you have listened to the five songs—now you have gone through ten—and you've moved up to a much higher plane of energy, climbing up the latticework of light, of dimensions—hold your attention on the third eye.

Your third eye, which is between your eyebrows and slightly above, the *ajna* chakra, is a center of knowledge. The third eye and the crown center, which is at the very top of the head, are the knowledge centers.

The three meridians are power, balance, which is happiness, and knowledge, or wisdom. When you bring all three together, you are complete.

There are five songs—the last five—that reference the higher chakras. Simply listen to them and keep your attention on the third eye. When thought comes in and out of your mind, ignore it. Simply listen to the music. Don't get frustrated if your mind is restless. There's a lot of energy in the world, and it takes patience to learn how to meditate.

What's happening as you listen to each song—the first five songs for the navel center, the second five songs for the heart center and the third five songs for the third eye—is you are bringing the kundalini up through concentration. The chakras are doorways to different dimensions, to different planes of enlightenment. As you hold your attention on them, the kundalini energy at the base of the spine will gradually rise—first to the navel center, then to the heart center, then to the third eye.

The crown center is a little bit different. It's not connected to the other centers. When you open it, you go into *samadhi,* into very advanced states of attention. It takes many, many years of practice to be able to activate the crown center, I wouldn't be too concerned about it at this time. Just bringing the kundalini eventually up to the third eye will release a tremendous amount of energy, brightness, beauty into your life. Your mind will become clear. Your life will become centered. You'll be able to use higher aspects of mind, have inter-dimensional experiences—and learn to be a little bit silly and smile about even very difficult things.

You'll gain knowledge and power. All kinds of wonderful things will happen just from meditating on these three chakras to the music.

As I said, there's an album for morning meditation and evening meditation. Optimally, you will do an hour of meditation in the morning and an hour in the evening—not necessarily at the beginning. In the beginning, you might just try meditating in the evening for half an hour once in a while or every day or in the morning.

But as you have progressively better and better experiences with meditation, you will find that it's good to meditate in the morning. When you meditate in the morning after you first get up, you energize your body, you wash out all the energies you picked up when you were very sensitive and your defenses were down—you know, during sleep. You clarify your mind. You gain mental power, control, and you release a lot of energy through the chakras, have inter-dimensional experiences—and you'll gain tremendous happiness.

Then during the day, you might say your auric immune system will be very powerful. You'll find it easier to keep thoughts and impressions that are negative out of your mind. Your mind will be clear and sharp. You'll do real well at school, in sports, at work, or just in having fun. You'll become more creative, balanced—instead of the person who just goes through the day without all that energy and all that clarity and just kind of makes it—you can be on top of things, in charge, and happily so.

Then, during the day, after your morning meditation, you should practice mindfulness. It's a fun game that you can practice all day long. All day, after you've meditated in the morning, as thoughts come in your mind—emotions, feelings—realize that most of them aren't your own. And just bounce out anything negative, anything negative, unhappy, angry, jealous, suspicious, anything that would make you unhappy and destroy your inner calm, your inner equilibrium that you've gained from your morning meditation. Just blow it out. Push it away. You gain the inner chi or power to do this from your morning meditation. If you keep doing this, eventually you'll find that you'll just be happy all the time. After a while, your mind just will automatically filter these thoughts out and negative impressions that you pick up from others, without even having to think about it very much.

We charge up our auric battery in the morning with a good meditation. Then in the evening, around sunset, or whenever you get home from the day, meditate again. Take a shower. Maybe go for a run—or whatever works for you—and meditate. Put on the *Canyons of Light* tape. It's a beautiful tape. Each of the songs references a power place in the Southwestern United States, an inter-dimensional vortex of power.

And during the day, of course, you will have used up a lot of the energy from your morning meditation, picked up impressions. Sit down. Meditate. Relax. Chill out. Be calm. Be centered. Be beautiful.

Eternity is around you and within you. Don't be afraid. There is only happiness beyond this world—the happiness, the endless happiness of nirvana and of the spirit. Relax. Trust life a little bit. What we see here is just a blink of the eye, this life. It comes and goes very quickly. There's much more to all of this, and it's much better.

Listen to the *Canyons of Light* tape. Allow it to guide you and take you through the 15 higher dimensions that it references. Start with the navel center—five songs there, the next five for the heart center, and the next five for the third eye. Remember, the key to success in meditation is to enjoy it, not to fight thought, but just to listen to the music.

You would normally learn to meditate, if things were ideal, with an enlightened teacher such as myself. You would sit, come and see your teacher twice a day and sit with them in the morning and evening. In the morning, you'd meditate together, and when an enlightened teacher meditates, it's very powerful. Their aura gets very charged up, and the pure power of their mind as they move from one chakra to another, from one dimension upwards into the planes of light and into samadhi and enlightenment and nirvana—as they do that, if your mind is at all subtle, if you practice meditation a little bit, the power of their aura will lift you along with them, from one plane of mind to another.

That's how you really learn to meditate. I mean, you just can't know where these planes are—how to get to them—just by trying by yourself. Enlightened teachers are there so that you can meditate with them and they move your mind from one plane to another. Then you can practice on your own and learn how to get back to those stages of attention, those wonderful worlds of light.

Normally you'd meditate with your teacher in the morning and later in the evening, and they would lift you into these higher planes. And by doing that repeatedly, day after day, month after month, you would learn—just as repeated motions in martial arts teach you the motions and the movements of martial arts—you would learn how to meditate.

What I have done is created two albums—there are others, but these two in particular, the *Enlightenment* tape and *Canyons of Light* on tape and CD—that are like having a private enlightened teacher. I have infused each of the albums with the light of enlightenment and with a tremendous amount of kundalini. The composition of the work actually came out of 30 different dimensions. And each song is actually—I can't explain how it's done—but let's just say that it's hooked up to a certain dimensional access point. When you listen to the songs, the level is actually there of a particular universe, a very high plane, and it will lift you up if you can just listen to it—into these higher dimensions, the same way it would if you were meditating with me or with another enlightened teacher.

When you put on the tape or the disc, essentially you're sitting down with an enlightened teacher and meditating with them. They're holding a plane for four minutes and you experience it as you focus on a chakra and you shift to another and another. Gradually, the kundalini rises from the base of the spine to the third eye, opening up the chakras, in the morning and of course in the evening.

After you meditate, after you finish the session, always bow. If you're sitting in the cross-leg position, if you can, touch your head to the floor. If not, you better lose some weight and do some exercises and limber up. If you're sitting in a chair, just bow slightly. We just like to offer our meditation to the universe. And sit still for a couple of minutes. Relax.

Never judge or analyze a meditation. Just do it. Focus as hard as you can on the chakras while you meditate.

Handy tips—avoid eating much before you meditate. Your body will feel heavy. It's like eating a lot before you exercise. Yuck. Relax. You're not going to learn how to do it in a day, but every time you meditate and simply listen to the music you'll go very high. You'll have a very beautiful experience.

When thoughts come in and out of your mind, ignore them. If you have experiences, see light, colors, sensations of lightness, that sort of thing, if cabbage grows out of your ears, don't worry about it. Just ignore it.

Experiences come and go in meditation, and, you know, let 'em go; let 'em come. What matters is that you just focus on the chakra undistractedly.

Another hint—disconnect the phone before you meditate. Everyone always seems to call you when you start to meditate. Put on the music and listen.

Zazen means to sit, to listen. You are listening to enlightenment, to the universes, to the planes of mind. You're sitting with an enlightened teacher, with enlightenment, more specifically. Let that enlightenment flow through you, purify you, clarify you.

With practice, you'll find that you get a lot better.

In the beginning, the music may actually distract you a little bit.

The music is very pure, though. Not only is it played by some of my students and produced and composed by all of us, but in addition, after the music is done, I take my aura and go through it and take out any human impressions, it's absolutely clean. It's perfect music in terms of its consciousness. And it's not bad, overall. We work hard on it; we really do, to make it for people, so they can have a beautiful experience.

Listen to the music. Meditate. Relax and just let it take you into the world of light, past other people's thoughts, other people's ideas and even your own.

There is nirvana. There is enlightenment. Beyond this world and beyond all worlds, there's something perfect and real. The comedies, the tragedies that we see played out on this earth before us don't last. But we are eternal spirits. We do. These events will come and go, but the planes of light and nirvana will always be there.

If you'd like to learn more about meditation and enlightenment, then you should find a teacher who you feel is balanced, powerful, knowledgeable, enlightened and funny. If they're not funny, they're not enlightened.

Trust life. Trust that it will always guide you to the right thing. And be kind. Be compassionate. Take time to help others and help yourself. Be patient.

If you meditate or—what Rama always says is—if you meditate each day and run each day, you can do anything. If you run a few miles and meditate every day, you're okay. That's in my opinion. But even if you miss the running, just get a little exercise any way you want to.

Meditate each day, and your life will get better. You'll be happy, free, successful and eventually you'll grow into pure and perfect light, into the world of enlightenment, and there is simply nothing better than that.

Please enjoy the music. We made it for you. And enjoy the tapes.

And grow, develop and always be optimistic. Always be positive. And ignore those who aren't because they're obviously confused and out of touch with light.

CHAPTER TWO

BUDDHISM

It's presumptuous for me or anyone to talk about Buddhism because it is so vast, it's so complete, and there are so many aspects of it. So without being presumptuous, I'll talk about Buddhism.

I'm an enlightened teacher, my name is Rama. I've been teaching Buddhism for lots of incarnations, and I teach it in this incarnation. But none of us really teach Buddhism. Buddhism is a way of life. It's yoga. And we practice it. People can watch us practice it; they can learn how to practice it by watching, by observing, by listening, by becoming sensitive. But I think it's something that life teaches us. We are teachers. We are necessary, but life is the real teacher and always remember that.

Buddhism is the enlightenment cycle, and there are different types of it. Principally there is short path and long path Buddhism. The long path is more of the religious aspect, that is to say, the church aspect, the practice of reading *sutras,* healthy ways of living, things like that—a certain amount of prayer, a little meditation. The esoteric aspect of Buddhism, which is short path Buddhism, is meditation. And I am a teacher of Zen and Vajrayana Buddhism primarily, which are the two primary short path forms of Buddhism.

The short path of Buddhism, which is kundalini yoga, involves the release of the kundalini energy through the chakras or energy centers to create very rapid enlightenment. It is also taught with empowerments from a teacher, someone who is enlightened, who has experienced paranirvana and gone through the gradated stations and stages of enlightenment and has the siddhas and powers necessary to utilize in the teaching process. It's a very complicated process.

The short path, of course, is the silly path. It's the path with the smiles. Because you have to be funny or you won't last long. It's about releasing energy. It's about being enthusiastic, overcoming all fears, doubts, worries and anxieties—basically being perfect all the time and knowing that you're not. That's Buddhism, the short path. The colophon is getting shorter all the time. Please put on a smile and a sense of humor if you're going to continue listening.

Buddhism is the enlightenment cycle, as I said before. It's about becoming enlightened. The essential premise of Buddhism is that there is enlightenment. There is nirvana. Beyond this world, beyond all worlds, there is something radiant, perfect and eternal. It creates these worlds and all aggregate formations. At the same time, it is beyond them. We call it nirvana. You could call it anything you wanted to—God, the Tao, Brahma, whatever you prefer—God, the names don't matter. It's that eternal reality which nothing can describe. It's beyond words.

Buddhism—yoga—is a practice. It's a way of yoking or joining your mind to that eternal reality and, at the same time, viewing this world and all worlds as particles of that reality. Buddhism is about living a very grounded, happy, fun life, being energized and being good at everything you do, and getting better constantly. It's about utilizing the full power of your mind, body and spirit—your emotions, everything—to enjoy life, to experience its multifaceted sides.

The essential practice in short path Buddhism is meditation. Meditation is a process in which you stop thought, transcend dimensionality and merge with a perfect light, through the planes of light and the causal worlds beyond the astral. And there you experience light. As you go into light for longer and longer periods, as you progress in your meditation practice, you transform. You become illumined. You overcome all limitation, all sorrow, all pain. You learn not to be bound by desire, and eventually you transcend death itself. This is the enlightenment cycle. It's the process of uniting your consciousness with eternity, of being eternal, eternally aware, and at the same time being poised, graceful, balanced and having a most excellent sense of humor.

What matters is the pathway. What matters is that you walk down it and enjoy it. If you are practicing Buddhism, if it's real yoga, then your life is better every day. That doesn't mean that better things happen to you. That's just life. Who knows what'll happen? It's an adventure. But if you are really practicing correctly, the litmus test to true practice is that you like yourself better. You like your life better. You feel better. You can see every month, every week, every year, an improvement in the states of mind you exist in, an improvement with how you handle both difficult situations and easy situations.

The best way to learn Buddhism is, of course, if you have an enlightened teacher, or if you don't have an enlightened teacher, a teacher who is much more advanced than yourself. There are two types of teachers: exoteric and esoteric. Exoteric teachers can explain the outer forms of yoga—how to conserve energy, gain energy, utilize that energy to go into higher planes of consciousness. They can explain practices, teach you all kinds of valuable things and techniques. But they don't have the transmutative power of the full kundalini. Only an enlightened teacher, an esoteric teacher, can actually empower you, transfer power from themselves to you so you can much more rapidly escalate your spiritual development.

If you are going to college and if you have a scholarship, or in graduate school if you have a fellowship, you can progress much faster. Instead of having to work a job and go to school, you can put all your time into school and get through a lot more quickly. Empowerments are designed to aid or speed the student's progress on the short path. Normally, it would take a much greater period of time to amass all the power necessary to go into enlightened stages of attention. But an enlightened teacher can actually transfer power to their students in the same way that a wealthy person can give somebody money. It's something tangible—power. You can't transfer knowledge. Not really. You can't transfer heart or the sense of loving things. You can expose someone to it. But you can transfer power—certain types of gradated kundalini. Part of the short path is the transfer of power. And this power is to be used to aid yourself and to aid others, never for anything destructive.

Buddhism is a practice in which we learn to avoid injuring others and ourselves. It's a practice in which we learn to respond to beauty and to respond to difficult circumstances with patience, with a sense of calm, with clarity—because we know we've lived before, and we'll always live in one lifetime or another; because you experience that in meditation. That knowledge and that power. We're not really afraid of things. We're not afraid of death. We're not afraid of life.

Needless to say, there are always people who will give you a hard time because you're a Buddhist or because you are an anything. We live in a world that's extremely dogmatic. And people don't understand. People on the earth are fairly simple, to be honest with you. I mean, they're still killing each other in wars and polluting their planet and yelling at each other and shooting each other, so how far along could they be?

Buddhism is a very comprehensive way. There's a lot of etiquette in it. There is a great deal of etiquette. Etiquette is an intelligent way of doing things. Over the centuries, ways of saving energy have been evolved by Buddhists, by people who practice yoga. And these methods are the etiquette of Buddhism.

Energy conservation is a very, very important part of the practice of yoga, of Buddhism. We only have only so much energy, and in order to exist in higher spheres of mind, you need more energy. Energy comes from releasing the kundalini through the practice of meditation. You gain energy that way. You gain energy through empowerments from enlightened teachers. You gain energy by going to power places, by making pilgrimages to sacred places where the earth vibrates faster. You gain energy by doing happy things, by being successful, overcoming obstacles and obstructions. That'll get your power up.

You gain power in strange ways, sometimes. I mean, in other words, things that you might not think release energy, do. Athletics, which you might think would just tire you out, actually releases certain types of kundalini. Certain foods have more energy than others. And there are ways to deal with life and with people—very intelligent methods so that you can co-exist with other people and not lose all your energy. Just because someone is in a bad mood, that doesn't mean they have to pull you into it. Just because someone's unhappy, that doesn't mean you have to be pulled into it. The etiquette of Buddhism is not—if it's a real practice—it's not bullshit. It's real. It helps you lead a better life. It helps you conserve energy so that you can live in higher states of mind.

The central practice, as I suggested, is meditation. And just in your overall understanding, you know, you keep hearing me say, "Well, Buddhism is yoga, yoga is Buddhism." Buddhism is not a singular way. It's a compilation of ways. And it's organic. It changes. It's a science of self-discovery. Buddhism is yoga. Yoga was started, who knows when, a long time ago, when the first person learned that they could still their thoughts and experience eternity and access the higher planes of mind and the spheres of perfection that exist in the mind of the universe, in the central nexus of nirvana.

Buddhism does not have a start and an ending. It was not started by any historical figure. It's a body of ways and beliefs and traditions which will enable a person, when practiced correctly, to experience enlightened states of mind. Occasionally, in each age and in different lands, a Buddha is born, that is to say, an enlightened person who simply recodifies in a new land. They recodify the ways, the practices; they make changes that are just intelligent, changes that adapt to a new century, a new culture. But Buddhism doesn't come from anybody. It exists by itself. It's the practice of becoming completely conscious. Overcoming depression, fear, anxiety, jealousy, the things that cause pain, attachment—and learning to exist in beautiful states of mind.

Buddhism is a way, and there are lots of forms of it, and you find a way that suits you the best. No way is better than another. There's short path, long path, Hinayana, Mahayana. There are many aspects to it. But the central point of all Buddhism is not the aspects, not the etiquette, not the books that have been written about it, but the practice of meditation. If you meditate, you're a Buddhist. Meditation is silencing the mind, making the mind still. Your thoughts are like a curtain that separate you from reality. When they stop, suddenly you can see eternity. The longer you can stop your thought, the deeper is your vision and your mystical experience, the deeper your journey into realities, into higher planes of consciousness and knowledge. The practice of meditation is something that you learn a little bit each time you meditate, a little bit more about.

You need to make your mind calm, quiet and still. That's the essence of all practice. Meditation is a letting go, a letting go of the ego into the clear light of reality. There's a higher light. In Buddhism we call it the *dharmakaya,* or the clear light, the suchness; the essence, we call it in Zen. It's there, ineffable and perfect. When you meditate, you allow that light to filter through your being, to come into your mind, body and spirit, and essentially to purify you. Just like bathing in a waterfall or taking a shower, it washes away the dirt and makes you clean. The light of enlightenment, the *dharmakaya,* that clear light, purifies all samskaras, all karmas, all experiences that you've had in this and other lives. It washes them away, energizes you and perfects you.

In Buddhism—you know, it's a funny thing to try and think about; you really can't. There is nothing that you essentially do in practice except stop thought. I mean, that's the ultimate. You might say Buddhism is about what you don't do. You don't think. You don't make stupid mistakes. You avoid them. You become conservative, concerned and conscious. Naturally you make millions of stupid mistakes. That's the learning process, and that shouldn't bother you. But the idea is to avoid real big mistakes by learning what's what, what reality is and what it's not, what practice is and what it's not.

Buddhism isn't about temples and incense and shaved heads and robes, and it's not about church. There are aspects of Buddhism that involve that, and I guess people enjoy that—that helps them. It strengthens their practice. But real Buddhism is about meditation. It's an individual experience. It's an individual journey into enlightenment. Someone else's journey may inspire you, but it won't enlighten you. You need to have your own journey into enlightenment. Each time you meditate, you are on the pathway to enlightenment. You are experiencing higher mind and higher light. You're a traveler, a mental traveler, on a journey which we call life. And death is not the end. It's just another step in the journey. The journey is eternal.

If you are interested in meditation in this lifetime, in Buddhism, you've probably practiced before. We're drawn back again in each lifetime to pick up where we left off. You may have a great deal of past life knowledge and power stored inside you, and the way you access it is by practicing meditation.

It's best to meditate twice a day, in the morning and the evening. If you meditate in the morning, you will energize your body, mind and spirit, clarify your purpose and just become happy. Then you're happy all day, successful all day. And then at night, meditate again and enter into the world of light. Fill yourself with light and you'll have a perfect night.

The central theme or theory of yoga or Buddhism is that happiness is not something that you really gain in the world. You know, in life we see most people trying to become happy through their careers, their relationships, their school, or athletics, hobbies, pastimes or whatever. Certainly a certain amount of happiness can be gained through those things, but also it would appear, judging from most people's experiences, that more unhappiness is gained than happiness. I mean, there aren't many happy people around. You don't see many smiles in the world.

Happiness does not necessarily come from experience nor knowledge. Yet there is happiness in knowledge. Happiness in knowledge, for sure, can come from meditation. There are worlds of happiness in knowledge outside of this dimension. Meditation is a way of getting to them. If you sit down in the morning and meditate, you will experience happiness, knowledge; you'll gain power. Then all day long you'll be happy. No matter what happens, you'll be happy. If you have a happy day, then great, enjoy it. But if you don't, you won't lose your happiness. You've stored it up in your morning meditation and then you'll gain more in the evening. Meditation puts an end to the dependency for happiness on physical things, on people.

If you love someone and they die, your life can be ruined. You can be miserable. But if you meditate, not so. Of course you'll experience sadness. That's natural, but because you meditate and you see that there is no death, and because you experience radiant happiness in your meditation and in the practice, you'll be happy no matter what happens.

This is a world where people age. They grow old, they die, they despair, their lives don't work out as they thought. Nothing seems to; it's a transient place. Things come and go fast, like youth, wealth, health. Visit an old age home. Visit a cancer ward. Things don't always work out so well. But if you're a Buddhist, if you practice, you can take these things in stride. Every year you grow older, you can grow wiser.

The West is a funny place. The East too, but I think the West is even funnier in certain ways. I like it, but it's strange. People here think that youth is what it's all about. This is the youth culture and old age is where we hide our old people away in homes, and they are stupid and sick and senile. What a weird concept. You see, in the Far East we feel that as people grow older, if they lead an intelligent life, they get more powerful; they get wiser, they become happier. But you have to lead an intelligent life. If you meditate and if you practice yoga, then your body shouldn't end up a mess at fifty or sixty or seventy. You should be mobile. You should be in good shape.

Most people use up all their energy and become old because they are stressed out, because they don't have any balance in their life. They're not grounded in happiness. They're not grounded in the spirit. If you practice yoga, if you meditate, do some exercising, lead an intelligent life, then every year you get older, every day that passes, you can become more enlightened, more aware, more conscious. That's the normal way. That's the healthy way. That should be everyone's way. Then there's no despair.

Old age isn't a time when you sit around and feel jealous about all these younger people who are running around in convertibles. I mean, that's not a problem. You did that; you enjoyed it; it was interesting, but it was facile. You were young then. You didn't have power then. As you grow older, you should be more intelligent. And you should enjoy what the kids do, but it's not what you do. You should be off having new adventures in different fields of attention. It's a more graceful way to be.

Buddhism and yoga are great practices because your whole life is streamlined. Your whole life becomes a way of achieving success, and it doesn't end at a certain age. It just gets better and better. But you have to stay centered in the practice.

Now there's a lot of confusion in the West and the East about meditation. Some people astral travel. They go into these kind of astral states above the body where they get spaced out and dissociated. And they think that's meditation. Not at all. Meditation is a beautiful and perfect state in which there is tremendous light, energy and humor. If you are not becoming happier, more centered and better at what you do in the physical world, if you can't relate better to people than you could before, if your conversation isn't sharper, you're not funnier, if you're not more street-wise, you're not meditating. You're spacing out. You're in the astral. And that is not meditation.

There's a kind of New Age-ism that you see in the West. You see it in the East too, where people walk around with a sort of dissociated look, and they think that they're being spiritual. There's nothing spiritual about being dissociated. That's just being dissociated. Spirituality is a graceful and beautiful state of mind. And it's sharp and very physical, too, in certain ways. I mean, martial arts comes out of Buddhism and yoga. And in martial arts—I also happen to be a martial arts teacher—in martial arts, you learn to use the body in a very dynamic and very graceful way, a very powerful way. Certainly, in martial arts, you know, you can't be spaced out or you're going to get a foot in the face. And I think that's a good way to look at Buddhist and yogic practice.

Buddhism and yoga make you funny, give you a sense of humor about life, about yourself. If you're becoming just a prig, or if you're getting spaced out, if it's about social climbing and who's who in the Buddhist set or sect, it's not Buddhism. I mean, they may call it that, but it's not pure practice. Pure practice is about the transcendence of ego, being clear, centered, being kind, being detached also in a positive way, leading your own life and not being afraid to, but always being a student, never being superior, meaning you know it all and there's no more to learn and there is nothing you can learn from anyone else.

There's no competition between teachers if they are really

Buddhists. There's only a smile between them of true acknowledgment that we're all in the world of light together, and how great that we practice, how great that there are other people who are having fun, too. When you see this egocentric competition between students and teachers, these are people in very early stages of practice. We have to allow latitude for that. I mean, you don't just become enlightened in a day or a week or a month or an incarnation. It's a beautiful process, but it takes a while.

Buddhism is about tolerance to an extent—having a tolerance in the practice with people who have trouble with it, who become egocentric, who turn it into politics, into a clique, into, oh, all the different things that can happen. In other words, by applying the vain human emotions in the ego to practice and energizing them with kundalini, one achieves nothing. This is about selflessness, stillness, flexibility and strength, wisdom and humor. These are human words, English words, that are trying to divine—define, interesting Freudian slip—trying to define spiritual states that are beyond words. But if you walk into a place where people are allegedly practicing yoga or Buddhism and you don't feel comfortable and they don't seem to be in touch, you're right. Time to go someplace else.

But then, sometimes, that's part of what students do. You go to a university for the teacher, not for the students, unless you're just looking for a social experience. If the teachers are great, they'll teach you what you need to know. Your university days will come and go, but if you learn something from your teachers, it'll help you your whole life.

In yoga and Buddhism, you look for the right teacher. There's no best teacher. There's no competition. There's the one that works for you. Good teachers are usually hard. That was my experience in college and graduate school. They're difficult, but they're understanding. They demand more from you so you can get more from yourself. But in Buddhism, there is a sense that the teacher is not responsible for your education. You are. In the West we feel if we come into a class, somehow the teacher—because we pay them—is supposed to educate us. Not so in the world of enlightenment. In enlightenment, you have to convince a teacher not only that you are worthy of teaching, but then that they should show you some of the secrets.

Buddhism is all about secrets, you know. And those secrets are things that most people don't learn because they are not enthusiastic enough or bright enough or patient enough or funny enough—or still enough. You have to have a yen for that which is infinity, for brightness, and you have to be willing to overcome your meanness and your separativity. You have to be flexible, open-minded. Then you have what we call the apprentice or the student spirit, the spirit of the young monk, or young monk-ess. Buddhism is something that you practice regardless of sex, religion, color, age—it doesn't matter. What matters is that you love light, that you want to learn and that you are willing to overcome your limitations.

There are those—in the West particularly, where Buddhism is not that well known, as I said before—who will give you a hard time because you practice. Employers will be bigoted. Some of my students and other students of other teachers have experienced that. There are nasty groups out there who try to put us out of business because we practice Buddhism, even in the good old USA. It has nothing to do with the Constitution—they're just the KKK of the spiritual world. They don't like it. Some people think of it as a third world religion. Next joke. Welcome to Japan, which is currently buying the world out of Buddhist-based mentality—we're a nation that's doing rather well if you check the yen.

Buddhism lends to good business, a good business sense, as not only the Japanese illustrate but as all Buddhists illustrate. It's a very sophisticated thing. But just, you know, the West is a very young culture. America is only a few hundred years old, and it's a great place, and I love it, and I enjoy teaching here. But there's not a lot of knowledge about Buddhism, one of the largest and oldest religions in the world. It is the oldest religion—yoga is, the oldest practice.

I do warn you, if you practice, that it does get a little rocky sometimes. People give you a hard time about it. But don't let it bother you. It's always that way in a new culture, in a naive culture. America's a great place. It's a wonderful place to practice Buddhism. The whole world is. And just as the Soviet Union and the demagogues who ran it fell apart, so all nations fall apart where there are demagogues.

Eventually light prevails. You just have to be patient.

So practice Buddhism. Learn to be enlightened. Put a smile on your face. Go find a great teacher. Meditate. And stay funny. That's the essence of all practices—enlightenment with a sense of humor. That's always the best.

CHAPTER THREE

POWER

Power is the active force in life. It is the force of life that makes awareness. Power is seen in the wind, in fire, in movement—physical movement, emotional movement, mental movement. Power is awareness. Power in Buddhism is defined very precisely in many different ways. There is no singular word that can encompass all the different aspects of power. The general term for power, spiritual power, the power of awareness, is *kundalini*. Kundalini is the energy of life that creates life. Life is awareness. It is movement. It is sentient.

Life is the power to perceive. Without perception, there is no life. Types of perception certainly vary. Plants have one kind of perception, amoebas another, birds another, human beings another, astral beings another. The universe itself is a giant perceptual matrix. It perceives itself in essence and through its substance. Buddhism, yoga, is the study of perception, and what is most endemic to perception is power—the power to exist, to perceive, and the power to change perception.

Perception defines everything. I may be sitting in a room and looking around, and I'll perceive the room in one way. Another person may be sitting in the same room and they will perceive the room in an entirely different way. They may have had a bad day—they're depressed, anxious, restless, and they don't enjoy being in the room at all. I may be sitting in a room very happy, maybe something great just happened, or maybe I'm just feeling good and the room is gorgeous. Its colors seem bright; the texture of the rug is vivid. The other person may not even notice these things. Their perception may be memory. Perhaps they're living right now in something that occurred earlier in the day that was unpleasant—maybe a confrontation with someone they knew well that was unpleasant.

Perception really varies. In other words, it's internal. Perception is emotive; it is mental; it has to do with thoughts. But it is, in its essence, what we are. That is to say, in a certain way we are what we perceive. Or you might say, what we perceive certainly defines what we are. Now, we have to think of life in reverse. If we are perceiving other than what we are, if perception is the awareness of other, certainly, perhaps in a sense, perception can be the awareness of oneself. But if, primarily, the way we view the universe is the universe as other than what we are, perception is a mirror. In other words, we are everything that we don't perceive.

All perception is a background. It's a screen through which we can see ourselves. Perception is the ability to become conscious of self and that which is other than self, and other than self is normally what we perceive—what you call the external universe. And who are we? Well, we are the being that perceives. And certainly without thinking about it, a distinction is made between who we are and what we perceive. We perceive that which is other and that which is self.

Power is the band that we perceive things on. In radio we have AM stations, FM stations, short wave stations and others. They're frequencies; they're megahertz, kilohertz—they vibrate. Frequencies vibrate at specific rates, and within those frequencies we transmit information and receive information. Perception is made up of bands. It's a way of talking about it. And the bands of perception vary greatly. There's the human band of perception, the mammalian band of perception that would include all mammals. There is the plant, invertebrate, and so on. There's lots of different bands of perception, and simply because we are in one band of perception and aware of it doesn't mean others are not there.

We may be listening to FM stations. That may be all we listen to. But thousands of AM stations are on a dial just a few vibrations away. Experiences are being had, people are transmitting information, listening to music, gathering information. It's just good to remember that the human field of perception is not in any way the only field of perception, the only band of perception. Nor is it necessarily the best. There is no such thing in infinity. Everything is the best, I suppose you might say. Infinity doesn't label—its creations are not labeled, they just are. Human beings like to label things and we like to say, "This is better than that; this is more pleasing; this is less pleasing"—according to our sensorial system or our mental or emotional system or philosophical, sociological or political systems or religious systems.

Power, to begin with, is the thing that holds a band of perception together, and a band of perception is life for those who perceive in that band. If that band of perception were to go away, they would not exist. And there are many great bands of perception in the universe. There are both organic and inorganic bands of perception. And today we're confining ourselves to the organic band of perception, specifically to the human band of perception. But I just want you to know that it is possible to modify your awareness field so you can perceive what plants perceive, what birds perceive, what beings in the astral perceive, what beings in the causal perceive.

There are many universes, many dimensions. They are endless. And it is possible to gain entry to those perceptual fields. Most of them are not particularly relevant for us. They won't help us. They won't make us happier. We won't gain knowledge or information or power that we can use to improve the quality of our lives. They simply don't reference it. There have been people who have classified and categorized these bands in different yogic systems. They enjoy—just as a botanist might enjoy classifying plants. It gives them some pleasure to create names and orders and to make catalogs. Human beings like that.

That's one function of intellect, is to catalog. But cataloging doesn't change anything. If we call it a rose, or by any other name, it smells as sweet. The name doesn't really matter. It's something that's convenient for us—to communicate with each other verbally or in written form what something is, or in pictorial representation, or in sound. But it really doesn't matter. In other words, if human beings didn't exist without all their categories and classifications, life goes right along down the street. Life is not dependent upon our classifications and our categories, our science. But we are. We find it interesting and helpful.

Power is the bands of perception themselves. Power is what holds the bands of perception in place. The ability to perceive what we call life, the ability to live, is one aspect of power. Without the power to exist, to perceive, there is no life as we know life to be. Then, more specifically, within the human banding of attention, let's say on the FM frequencies, there's lots of variation. We can go from the bottom of the dial to the top of the dial. Or we can change bands completely and go to AM or short wave or an even longer wave.

Within the human frequency, well, what you see is what you get. There are the different conditions, mental conditions, awareness conditions, that you see people on earth existing in. They're relatively representative. I would classify the bottom of the band as severe unhappiness, depression, alienation—things that we would consider very unpleasant. The top of the band, which would vibrate a little faster, would be happiness, contentment, peace of mind, a feeling of balance and overall wealth of spirit and ecstasy.

Buddhism, yoga, is concerned primarily with moving our

awareness field from the beginning of the band of perception, the human band, up to the top, and eventually, of course, going from the human band to an enlightened band, or bands, of perception—just leaving this band of perception completely. But before you do that, you have to move through the human band from wherever you happen to be to the top. You can't go beyond until you get to the top.

You were born with a specific awareness field. And that's your *karma*. Karma means who you are, that is to say, where your awareness field is on the band of perception. And in past lives, whatever you did or did not do, whatever you experienced or did not experience, has caused you to be at a certain wavelength, to have a certain awareness field. When you're born, that awareness field is not completely at your disposal. We may have a book that someone wrote and it may be in our hands and it may have all kinds of information in it, but until we've read it we don't have the information. We can't reference it or utilize it or enjoy it.

Within us is all the information from all the lives that we've led. And simply being alive doesn't mean we've read the book. One aspect of Buddhism, or inner study, is the reawakening of past life knowledge, and it takes a certain type of power to do that. Past life knowledge is not necessarily a remembrance. It's not the wedding album photo scrapbook of existence. You can remember what you did last week, and it doesn't necessarily change anything, the physical events. Past life remembrance in Buddhism means the ability to bring a greater awareness, a greater knowledge that we had in another life into this life. The actual memories of where we were in time and space and with whom are not usually relevant.

If you were a great architect or a great musician in a past life, if you could bring that knowledge, that overall sensitivity, let us say, that you developed through architectural design and music into this lifetime, you'd be way ahead of the game—if you wanted to pursue those things in this life. But when you're born or as you grow up—until you have a certain type of power, a certain type of kundalini—you cannot reference, you can't get access, you can't dial-in to those things.

One aspect of power is the power to bring our total awareness into this lifetime. A second aspect of power, of course, is to go beyond that awareness, the things that we've known in other lives, into new fields of awareness that we've never experienced. And the very transmutative energy or power that does that is called the kundalini. The kundalini is the energy that opens up the bands of perception. It's also the energy or power that enables us to travel, mentally, from one level to another, from one plane or dimension to another, from one experience to another. It's also the energy that enables us to have what I call a weird power, to do things or make things happen that would not happen otherwise, to apply a pressure, an occult pressure—in other words, to use energy backstage—to be able to use energy that is invisible to most people to create effects, perhaps thousands of miles away from where your body is located, or in other dimensions—to heal, for example. If you have power, you might be able to heal a person who has a disease without having to resort to antibiotics or surgery or whatever might be necessary. You could actually get inside their cell structures and create a change. You might be able to mold and shape events in your life or the lives of others.

Power is something that is not really visible—the kind of power that I am speaking about. It exists, certainly. We can see it in human life. Some people have the power to rise above circumstances. They went to the same high school with everyone they knew. They grew up in the same kind of environment, were exposed to the same materials, but for some reason they got to the top of the class. They succeeded in a way that most people didn't, just even externally—perhaps in a material sense, perhaps in a spiritual sense, a political sense, a philosophical sense. Certainly the sociological factors and DNA are not all that determine success. It's power, past life power or current life power that we gain through the practice of meditation, by leading a relatively conservative but extremely exciting and happy life—conservative in terms of the usage of energy.

Buddhism, one aspect of it, deals exclusively with power—how to get power, store power, utilize it intelligently, so that it creates benefit to oneself and to others. The primary energy that's active in all the things that I've been discussing is kundalini. Kundalini energy is the energy of awareness and it can be used to modify awareness. An example might be an intelligent atom—perhaps that's a way of looking at it. If an atomic structure—protons, neutrons, valances, electrons—could become aware of itself, and if it had the knowledge, it could change itself. It could add maybe some different electrons to some of its valances, change its atomic number by changing the protons and neutrons. If it had the ability to do that, it could become something other than it was.

Human beings do that in a way, all the time. We are born with a physical defect but we've gained the knowledge to change our body. We can perform surgery. We can have a radiation treatment. We've learned to use certain medicinal drugs to heal ourselves, to change our condition. We can go to school and gain knowledge and better our lives, have a different career. In a sense, we do that all the time. We're intelligent atoms, I suppose. We're intelligent organic structures. We can change who we are. And now, of course, even as you know, with genetic engineering, they're beginning to look at the possibility of changing the actual physiological structure of the body—first, perhaps, in small ways with synthetic drugs that they're creating and manufacturing; but eventually, perhaps, in larger ways.

Buddhism, yoga, is the study of changing who we are, modifying or perhaps totally restructuring ourselves as perceivers. Now, in a way, you really can't change who you are. Whoever you are is who you are, and that always will be. There's something in us that's eternal, and that's beyond change. And the ultimate goal of Buddhism is to reach that from this side, to become conscious of that side. This side is the mortal side, the limited side, the human side. Then there's the eternal side, the timeless, divine side. And we seek to, in yoga, to yoke or unify our awareness field with the divine or enlightened side, the timeless side—because when we do that there's no pain, there's no anxiety, there's no unhappiness. The eternal part of our being is perfect, free, always changing, always new, and completely conscious of all things—complete aliveness, complete awareness.

However, in the meantime, and on the way there, Buddhism is the study of power, initially. It takes a certain amount of power to even know your potential—to have a sense that you can change the way you perceive, what you perceive and that it will be very beneficial to you. It takes additional power to find out how to do that and even more power to actually do it. And of course, when you make structural changes in perception, it gives you power. It's very curious the way it all works. It's not necessarily logical. It just is how it is. Things are not necessarily logical. Logic is a way of looking at something. It's a flow chart, a mental flow chart. But everything is not logical. Things just are. And logic is a secondary source referencing where we look at something and say, "Oh, well, this is this way because ... " No, it's not. It is what it is. And we've decided that we want to apply rationale to it. It makes us feel better.

The power that is most interesting is the personal power that changes or shapes consciousness, and that's kundalini. Kundalini exists everywhere. It's called *shakti,* another name for it. That is to say, it's a latent energy field, an invisible energy that is present in all of life, everywhere, in this dimension and in other dimensions. Then, more specifically, kundalini exists within us. It exists in greater amounts in certain places. Some people have more of it. Some dimensions have more of it. And initially, the student of Buddhism seeks to become aware that there are variations or differences in power. Some people have more than others. Some places have more than others. Some activities create and give one power. Some are draining. Some take power away. Since power is necessary to go into the happier states of mind and sustain them, to stay in them, and to go beyond them to the enlightened states of mind, which is, of course, the most desirable thing; since power is necessary to be healthy, to heal one's body, to assist others, it's the primary concern. It's the first face on the totem pole in self-discovery.

Kundalini in a human being rests in potential at the base of the spine. We have a physical body, and we have a subtle body and a causal body. And then, of course, there is the eternal part of ourselves. There's a touch of nirvana in all of us, something that is non-physical, non-dimensional, non-astral and non-causal—the real in us—but it is obscured. It's hard to get to because of the physical body, the emotions, the thoughts, the mind, and just in general because we don't have enough power to perceive properly. Kundalini is at the base of the spine.

The *subtle physical body* surrounds the physical body. It's a body of energy. It's also known sometimes as the *astral body.* And it's composed of chakras, energy fibers, astral tubes that are similar to veins. Basically, the part of the subtle body that concerns a practitioner of yoga and Buddhism is the *shushumna.* The shushumna is a tube. It's an astral tube. It's kind of like a reed that runs from the base of the spine to between the eyebrows and a little bit above. And there are six chakras or energy vortexes that lie along the tube. The first is at the base of the spine. The second is the area around the spleen or the sex organs. The third is about an inch below the navel center. The fourth is in the center of the chest. The fifth is in the throat, the base of the throat. The sixth and the topmost chakra or energy center on the shushumna is between the eyebrows and about an inch above. There's a seventh chakra which is located several inches above the top of the head, but it's not connected to the others directly.

There are many other chakras, or *nadis* as they are also called. There are chakras in the hands, fingertips, feet and a number of other areas. They're not really in the physical body. If you lost an arm it wouldn't affect the subtle body or the chakras. They are non-physical. They're astral. But they are in approximately that same area. It's a way of trying to talk about them.

The release of power, the power that enables us to transform our awareness, to be successful and happy in life, is the release of the kundalini. All yoga either directly or indirectly, all Buddhism, relates to the release of the kundalini energy. The kundalini energy is in the first chakra at the base of the spine. It is called the root chakra. And through meditation, through going to certain places, being around certain types of people, participating or not participating in certain types of mental or physical or emotional activities, it's possible to take that energy and allow it to move, to unleash it, from the base of the spine up to the third eye and eventually to the crown center. This energy, as it moves, it's often compared to a snake that is coiled up and it seems kind of small, but because it is coiled it can spring very quickly. It can just jump and extend itself very fast.

The kundalini is seen as a serpent, as a coil of energy that's at the base of the spine, but it can shoot right up through the shushumna, pass through the chakras, opening them all and bringing you into different states of awareness and finally bridge the gap and enter the crown center. The crown center, also known as the thousand-petal lotus of light, references the dimensions or planes of light, of enlightenment. Each of the seven chakras references different dimensional planes. That is to say, it's a doorway. It's a turnstile that leads us into different dimensions. And as the kundalini rises, either in an individual meditation session or just the general level in your life, those dimensions will be opened to you and the knowledge and powers of those dimensions will begin to come to you.

There is an immediate rise and there's a general level. The general level is where the kundalini abides most of the time. In most people, the kundalini is in the first chakra. It may be in the second. That is to say, if we were to measure their kundalini, if we could look at it, we would see that it's in the first or somewhere between the first and second chakra for most people on earth—usually in the first. It's pretty locked up. And for average people who don't practice Buddhism and yoga, the kundalini only becomes active maybe a few times in their life. At times of extreme intensity, the kundalini can become active. Very unusual circumstances—a car accident, emotional trauma, sometimes in warfare, in a battle situation—something can cause the kundalini to suddenly come out and when it does, it gives a person incredible power. Suddenly they can overcome all fear and attack the enemy because one of their friends was wounded and, you know, be very successful. Suddenly a 70 year-old lady who can't lift a bag of prunes will lift up an automobile several inches because her grandchild got stuck under it.

You know, the kundalini can do physical things. But it can do mental things. It can make us understand something that we wouldn't understand. If someone we love dies, and normally the experience might be horrifying or create misery for the rest of your life. But the kundalini can be released, and it brings us to a higher level of knowledge and understanding, and we see that there is no death, that that person has just gone, like we all must, on a journey. We'll be following them soon. We've all been on it before. We'll all be on it again.

It can provide mental awareness, a scientific discovery, a musical creation, all kinds of things. People who tap the kundalini and are able to release it are more successful in their chosen fields of endeavor—great painters, musicians, architects, scientists, engineers, philosophers, martial artists, whatever it may be, athletes. Anyone who is really on top has some access to the kundalini. They may not practice what they would call meditation every day and sit down formally and meditate and focus on the chakras, but they have learned somewhere along the line, in this life or other lives, ways of releasing power. And then they can use that power in a variety of ways, depending upon how wise they are and how balanced they are.

Whenever you see someone who has reached the apogee of their profession—if you are dealing with someone who is a corporate head of a very substantial corporation, if you see someone who is a very fine musician, a great writer, what we would call someone eminently successful in one or more fields—is someone who has what I call a weird power. That is to say, they've learned how to unlock the kundalini. There are things they do, there are foods they eat and don't eat, places they go or don't go, thoughts they think or don't think, emotions they experience or don't experience. Just the way they hold their mind, in other words, they've learned—although they wouldn't call it meditation or yoga—how to meditate. And they consciously release the kundalini, or unconsciously.

Obviously, if you learn to consciously release the kundalini, you can be more successful even than those people are. Because they have come across something that they know works. They can't tell you how in most cases. They know there is just something they do that keeps them on top of their profession, makes them happier, makes them more successful. But they don't know where they can go from there, you might say. They've taken this as far as they can, and they just keep doing it over and over. But in yoga, in Buddhism, you study how to release and unlock the kundalini and take it up to the levels that would certainly afford career success, personal happiness, and physical health and mental balance. But we move it further into planes of knowledge and wisdom that enable the practitioner to do just about anything. In other words, there are ranges of experience and ecstasy—just plain fun—that people don't even know are there to get to. Consequently they don't. Or if they did, of course, they wouldn't know how to do it or be able to do it unless you practice yoga or Buddhism or something similar in which there's an actual study of the structures of awareness—how to transmute them properly and intelligently, with wisdom and balance. That's the study of power.

Power is something that's abused, something that's used. I suppose use and abuse are in the eye of the beholder. But I would say, essentially, my template for viewing use and abuse is happiness. Happiness is not the same as pleasure. Pleasure is an immediate experience, very transient in nature, that's enjoyable. And if we experience a great deal of it, there's a sense of satiation. After you have too much pleasure, you actually don't feel good.

On the other hand, happiness is something that the more you have of it, the better off you are. There is no such thing as too much happiness. It doesn't satiate.

I would define the proper use of power as something that creates happiness for yourself and for others. And the abuse of power takes happiness away. It's the enemy of happiness. Everything that I teach as a Buddhist teacher, as an enlightened Buddhist teacher, is towards directing an individual to happiness—not just a pleasurable experience or the avoidance of a painful experience but towards a happiness, a balanced wisdom and knowledge that's sometimes just bubbly and euphoric or just very deep, very quiet, very still, very profound. The less we define it, I think, the better.

Power, however, doesn't create happiness or unhappiness. It just is. It depends how you use it. Wisdom is the guiding force that directs happiness. Balance is happiness. It's the ability to not need to go further today, to be satisfied and just to be bright—not to avoid, not to overdo, but just to enjoy.

Power is abused when its uses create unhappiness. And in particular, the abuse of power that seems to create the most unhappiness is when a person uses personal power to get ahead without regard to the welfare of others, or when power is used to go into the lower dimensional planes. These are the primary abuses of power, and if you learn them and avoid them, then you'll have a very happy life in your practice of Buddhism.

Power can be used to get ahead. You can use power to get things other people can't get, once you unlock the kundalini. You could go into an interview situation for a job, and you could cause someone else not to get the job. You could focus on them and they just wouldn't perform well that day. People do this a great deal. A student of mine is an actor and he goes to auditions for films, for film parts. And very often before the audition, he's sitting in a waiting room with a number of other actors and actresses who are trying to get the part. And he observed, after he had become more aware of power and how it's used, that some of the people there would use their energy field simply to throw somebody else offline so that they wouldn't do well in the interview. They might talk to them for a while, pretend they're their friend or whatever, and at the end of the conversation the person was completely exhausted, drained—they'd go in and do a terrible audition.

People have power and it's very important to respect that. The way I look at it is—everybody's had thousands of lifetimes, if not more. And who knows what anyone has learned in a lifetime. Respect is not fear. Respect is an intelligent apprehension. And I think it's a good idea to have respect for all beings because who knows what anyone knows or can do?

My student used to go into these interviews, as I said, and sometimes not get a film part because he would be "taken out." Someone would use power in a way that would cause him not to succeed. Now, needless to say, while the person might have gotten the part, they would be unhappy in their own personal life because when we use power—this is the hardest thing to explain or teach, I think, in life—when we use power to cause someone else not to succeed so that we can succeed, it slows our vibratory frequency. It slows us down. We vibrate at a certain rate, each one of us. And when the rate speeds up, we experience happiness. We go higher on the band. When it slows down we experience unhappiness, and we go further down on the band.

Now the point of life, what makes life worth living, is happiness. Success does not necessarily create happiness. I could take you on a tour of West Los Angeles or any other very wealthy area, where you'd go into homes and meet people who are very successful in their careers, in the amount of money they make. And you'd be surprised that happiness does not blossom in Beverly Hills any more than it does in most places.

Happiness has to do with how quickly you vibrate, how intelligent you are, how subtle your awareness field is, how deep you are, how aware of your eternal part you are. That's what creates happiness. Pleasure just comes from a temporary working out of things in a way that you like. But it doesn't last. As soon as circumstance changes, you're unhappy if it doesn't change in a way that you consider favorable. Happiness is endemic. It's part of us. And Buddhism is the process of getting to that part of us that is always eternally happy, bringing that happiness into our physical and mental and emotional life and experiencing it, enjoying it and knowing it.

Meditation is a process of speeding up the vibration. When you meditate, you increase your own energy level. With that increased energy level, through the stoppage of thought and a variety of other things, you can succeed or you could cause someone else not to succeed. I personally don't feel that the answer is to cause others not to succeed in order that you can succeed. It's better to take the increased energy of meditation and just put it into your own success and not try and use it to cause others to fail. Because if you put it into your own success, you'll be happy whether you succeed or not, and chances are you'll succeed.

And this is what I suggested to this actor-movie star student of mine, that he simply not be concerned about this—know that it's going on; it's good to know the street—and that he utilize his full energy from his practice of Buddhism and yoga to simply do the best that he could, to be at the highest energy level, best level of performance that he could. But needless to say, to be conscious that there are people who do what we'd call, I don't know, black magic, lower sorcery. There are people who use power to interfere with the success of others, and not to be concerned about them. They're not happy people, and they can't necessarily be any problem to you as long as you're aware of what they're doing. You just step around them. When he was waiting to go on and be successful and to get the film part, I would suggest to him that he simply avoid those people. Just look around the room, and if you see this is what people are doing—they're spending most of their time and energy causing each other not to succeed—rather than do that, just to take a book with him, to sit and read it, something that would raise his energy level, to ignore everybody, keep his energy that he gained—from his life and his hard work and his meditation and the practice of his craft—in his body and then simply to go in there and do a great audition. To get involved with some ridiculous battle of power with someone else will use up his energy, and then he would go in and not have much energy to succeed.

In other words, the trick is simply to avoid jerks, in my opinion, in life. There are lots of them out there. Most people are unhappy, intrinsically it seems, and there are people who just go their own way, and then there are people who just seem to want to trouble you. And so, intelligent martial arts is not getting in battles and winning them. Intelligent martial arts is avoiding battles because battles use up energy, and you can get hurt no matter how good you are, and that wasn't what you had on your agenda today. Simply because you were going someplace today and you were going to have a great picnic, and you didn't intend to get in a battle with somebody, if you get in a battle and even win, you never get to have your nice picnic. That was somebody else's idea. The intelligent use of power is to apprehend those who would trip you up, to slide around them and go do what you want to do. Naturally, if there is no way out and confrontation and battle is inevitable, one can use power and strategy, balance and wisdom and enlightenment to win, of course. But the best battle is the battle that's never fought. The best war is the war that's won without battle.

But it is important to know that power can be used to interfere with things. To be afraid of that, however, is absurd. In other words, I have seen people who practice yoga and Buddhism who are scared to death of the sorcery powers of others, and this is absurd. If you are afraid of someone, you immediately give them an advantage over you and you give them entry to your awareness field. People can't do much to one another with power, in my opinion, by and large. Most people—they're not far enough along, they don't have enough of it or know how to use it properly. I wouldn't be very concerned about this. I think it's paranoia. What you can do, though, is allow someone to upset you. And if you become afraid of someone, they do gain a power over your life.

I think a lot of people profess to have power, and it's very minor astral power, and they get people very upset and then they do get power over you, not because they had any intrinsic power but just because your fear immobilizes you and makes you do a bad job. People can drain your energy a little or maybe they can make you feel a little bit uncomfortable. By and large, that's about it. That's what you are going to find around here, particularly in the West. And you know, at the most you're going to get a headache. But if you become afraid, well then, anyone can overwhelm you and totally dominate your life.

The intelligent use of power is never to interfere with anyone else's success, but to use the greater power you get to just be more successful yourself. Use power to intelligently apprehend people who might mean harm to you, and use that power to not be afraid, to simply step around them. And that's the end of the discussion.

Use power to vibrate more quickly. There is enough room in this world for lots of people to succeed. Your success does not depend upon the failure of others. The way to win the race is not to trip somebody else in the race, but it's to train hard, to feel great about yourself and to simply have more energy than other people do because you practice better yoga and Buddhism. That's my opinion. Because you will not only have a greater chance of winning, but whether you win or lose you're happy. Whereas, what is the great joy in winning some victory if it makes you miserable? It's no victory. It's a failure.

I don't put much stock in powers that people have to hurt others, in sorcery and all this nonsense. I think there are a lot of unhappy people trying to make other people unhappy, and sure, people have oppressive natures, and sure, there are people who are horrible and who kill and hurt people physically. There are murderers and there are dictators and people are out of control, their desires are obsessive or they are just lost in illusions. That's just part of life. But the intelligent use of power in yoga can assist you in avoiding that side of life and that side of humanity. And if you have to come into a battle, you can win it.

But what yoga does is—it makes you free. It makes you happy. And it gets you out of all the traps of human nature that create misery. Power's best use then, the correct usage of power, is for one's own personal success, and if you enjoy it—it's not necessary—to make others succeed. You might find that makes you even happier. It adds to your power. It makes you vibrate faster.

But the key line, the benchmark, is happiness. And in practice, that is to say, in the practice of meditation, Buddhism and yoga, what is necessary or required is to simply extend your happiness to higher and deeper levels today than it's been on any other day of your life. I would say if you're doing that, you're getting A's in Buddhism. And if you are not doing that, if you are at the same level, you are getting C's. And if you are not as happy as you used to be at any point in your life, you are definitely failing the course, which means you're not practicing properly. There's a bug in the program. We have to read the code—we have to look back and see what it is. It's not by accident. There is no such thing. You are not doing something. And chances are, you are not meditating properly, deeply and fully. You may be trying to skip steps and circumvent the process. You are using power incorrectly. Your motives are not pure. You don't vibrate quickly.

It's simply a question of doing a system analysis of your energy flow, spotting where the problem is and changing it—without a sense of ego, without a sense of right or wrong—I was good, I was bad—guilt or remorse. These things are unnecessary. It's just simply structural.

Everything in Buddhism is structural. Emotions are there to enjoy life, but they're not used in self-reflection because they inhibit a proper reflection. They gunk us up. Feeling sorry for yourself is a total waste of time, as is feeling sorry for others. Compassion and empathy are not the same as feeling sorry for oneself. They are emotions that extend our perceptual ranges. Whereas feeling sorry for yourself, feeling guilty, this accomplishes little or nothing in terms of a true change, an improvement of our state as perceiving beings.

The unlocking of the kundalini, which occurs by meditating on the first, second and third chakras, is the entrance into the planes of power. As you focus on the first, second and third chakra, you will gain access to the planes of power, and with planes of power, of course, come not only power, but experience in those dimensional planes. By and large, the first two planes are somewhat tricky for the beginner in meditation. Meditating on the first chakra and second chakra is not necessarily recommended. If you don't have enough power, the planes won't access or open anyway, and you won't get anything from the experience. And if they do, there can be very powerful releases of energy that can kind of catch you off guard until you have a better sense of what you are doing. If you're a new swimmer and you're swimming in the ocean in big waves, you might have an unpleasant experience or drown. If you learn to swim and gain self-confidence in a pool or in a place where there aren't huge waves, then later on you can learn how to deal with the waves, and they're actually kind of fun.

I would recommend, initially, if you are trying to increase your personal power level, to devote a third of your meditation practice to meditating on the navel center, not the lower two. The navel center will activate the other two centers, but the particular planes it references are relatively easy to deal with and they bring the full power of all of the three lower centers into your being. You gain the power without the problems. Later on in the enlightenment cycle, it is necessary to learn how to go out and surf some bigger waves. And it's fun. But initially, why look for a difficult experience? Seek a pleasant experience. You won't gain more power from focusing on the first two chakras than you will from the third. The third picks up all three. When you focus on the third chakra, it has to pull the kundalini from the root center through the second up to the third chakra.

There are places of power, places where there is more power. Just as there's more power in the chakras, there's more power in certain areas. We call them "places of power"—in the Southwest United States, in certain mountains, deserts, sometimes by the sea. Sometimes where they build a city or even a shopping mall, there are places of power. In the United States we're fortunate. We have a lot of places of power, particularly in the Southwest. Naturally in the Himalayas; there are lots of places of power in India. In Japan there are a number of places of power, very strong places. Mt. Fuji, of course, is a very strong place of power, and so on and so forth. There are lots of places of power around the earth. And if you spend time in these places, it increases your vibratory power. If you meditate in them, you can have very deep, profound experiences and store a lot of power.

Pilgrimages are journeys to places of power. Places of power very often have been frequented in the past by practitioners. For example, if you were to go to the Himalayas, people make pilgrimages sometimes to the caves where Milarepa and other great yogis meditated—not simply to pick up the energy or the vibration of the people who meditated there but because the place was and is intrinsically powerful, and that's why Milarepa and others were meditating there.

The Indians in the Southwestern United States went to many places of power. And in those places of power, they were able to have profound dream experiences where they could see the future or know what to do and make proper decisions, where they could just be more and feel more and know more. Power places in the United States are certainly not limited to the Southwest. There are a number of them in the East, and in the South, and in the Midwest. But the majority of them are in the Southwest—the power planes. You might say, in a way of speaking, that these places reference the first three chakras. There are physical places that reference the fourth and fifth chakra—the chakras of balance. And there are places that reference the sixth and seventh chakra—places of wisdom. That's what you have out there. There are negative places also that can drain your energy. They just vibrate really slowly. They're weird, and when you are in them, they just pull you down.

We're talking about keeping ourselves in a pure flow of light, being happy, learning to access and utilize power to clarify our minds, strengthen our bodies, renew our spirits, and generally have an experience of ecstasy, exultation and wisdom in the world of enlightenment. It's power that makes all this possible. Without power, none of it happens. There is no life without power.

The last consideration in our short journey through the world of power is the teacher of Buddhism. There are two types of teachers of Buddhism: exoteric and esoteric. Again, I am using the terms of Buddhism and yoga interchangeably. The exoteric teacher of Buddhism is someone who doesn't have power, really. They have a certain level of knowledge. It's a person who has meditated perhaps for some years and practiced Buddhism. They can show you basic techniques of meditation. They can show you things that they've learned from their teacher or just doped out themselves or learned from books about how to save energy, how to increase it to a certain extent. They've reached a higher belt ranking in the inner world perhaps than the student has, the new student. But they don't have true power. They may be able to make a person feel a certain amount of energy or shift their awareness slightly. But they don't have the knowledge and the balance necessary to be an esoteric teacher—and the pure power.

An esoteric or enlightened teacher of yoga and Buddhism is someone who has obviously attained enlightenment, and has the ability to transfer—just as you'd give somebody money, if you had a lot, if you made a lot—they have the ability to transfer power to another individual, to someone they might meet or usually to one of their students. These are called, needless to say, empowerments. A real empowerment is not just a ceremony. In order to do an empowerment, a person obviously has to be highly empowered, have the power and also have the structural knowledge of how to transfer it to someone else. There are lots of ways to do it. It's a very complicated thing.

The reason that you study with a teacher, as opposed to just pursue Buddhism and yoga on your own, is primarily for the empowerments, for someone who is enlightened and powerful to transfer power to you on a regular basis. Because with transferred power, you can go faster into the world of enlightenment. If you have a scholarship and you are going to college or graduate school, you can devote more of your time to studying and progress faster and do a better job with your scholastic endeavors. If you have to go out and work 30 hours a week at a fast food place, you might learn some interesting things and eat a lot of burgers or whatever, or fries, but you're not going to be spending time you could be spending on your schoolwork.

Teachers transfer power to their students so that a student is able to progress faster. They can meditate better, maybe be more successful in their career so that they can spend a little less time on it and have more time to meditate and do other things. They might heal them in some way, help them with their physical body. There are millions of applications for power. But what's most important is that the student uses that power intelligently and wisely. The primary reason for studying with an enlightened teacher is that they give you power. And with that power, the kundalini becomes active and moves through the chakras much more rapidly, and you are able to see and operate on levels that you would not maintain on a regular basis.

As I said earlier, there is a normal kundalini level that most people have which is either in the first chakra or somewhere between the first and the second. An enlightened teacher has all seven centers open all the time. Their kundalini is always all the way at the top. In an individual meditation session, we raise the kundalini to a degree for a short time—even though our normal level is first or second chakra, we may bring it up to the fourth or fifth, or maybe even the sixth level. But it'll only stay there for a few minutes and then it will recede. Gradually, doing that again and again—gradually, over many days and months—the level changes on a regular basis and we exist in higher kundalini levels all the time.

When you study with an enlightened teacher, they do individual empowerments when you see them. But if you're an accepted student of theirs, they are always transferring a certain degree of power from their aura to you. Instead of living between the first and second chakra, you might live in the third or fourth chakra all the time, or perhaps even higher. It depends on how adept and adroit you are with the usage of the power transfer. Transferring power does a lot of different things. It enables a person to be successful, to be personally happy, to be materially successful, to be spiritually successful. But it's not all we go to a teacher for—we also go to a teacher to learn balance and wisdom.

Without balance and wisdom, power becomes very destructive. It creates unhappiness and not happiness. And to simply see a teacher to gain power is a mistake. You'll gain the power, but with the current mindset that you have, you'll probably create more unhappiness for yourself than happiness with it.

We see an enlightened teacher to gain a sense of humor, to learn balance and proportion and, of course, to learn wisdom; to learn to intelligently cultivate the higher mind and to only use that power that the teacher transfers to us and, of course, also teaches us to develop for ourselves through meditation and certain practices; to use that power to succeed and create happiness and not to block the success of others; to gain emotional control, mental control, physical control and spiritual control so that we can hurtle ourselves into the most beautiful states of mind—into ecstasy, into enlightened states of mind where we can become one with the eternal part of ourselves; and to avoid blocking others, interfering with others because that will decrease our happiness, slow our vibratory rate and generally bring us down and make us miserable.

A teacher teaches you—an enlightened teacher—how to use power, how to gain power. They give you power. But they teach you how to shape it so that it becomes an instrument of beauty and not an instrument of unhappiness; an instrument of fulfillment and higher experience, and not an instrument of self-frustration or the frustration of others.

Use power very carefully. Don't be afraid to have it. You have to have it to succeed. But learn balance and wisdom in addition simply to the unlocking of the kundalini, if you wish to have a happy and enlightened life.

CHAPTER FOUR

BALANCE

Spiritual balance is the ability to be happy in spite of circumstances. Spiritual balance is the obvious answer to the obsession that sometimes accompanies religious practice, occult practice, philosophical understandings. The obsession, the assertion that one is right, that something that you're doing is better than something somebody else is doing, that the way you're doing it is better than the way someone else does it.

Spiritual balance is how you deal with opposition, opposition outside of yourself and opposition within yourself. Spiritual balance is *tai chi*. It's the center of things. It's the place where *yin* and *yang* meet, where all things come together. In the chakras, it's considered the heart chakra, *anahata,* the central chakra—three above and three below—which symbolizes happiness and love, psychic oneness, spiritual understanding.

Pure and simple, balance is happiness—happiness in spiritual practice, happiness while meditating, happiness while working, while playing, in pleasure and pain, in sickness and in health, in life and in death, in all circumstances. That's balance.

How do you do that? How can you be balanced in a world like this? You've got to be kidding, right?

Well, the world has always been this way, at least in one form or another. I mean, I'm sure in the Middle Ages, or in the ancient Chinese civilization or the mystery world of Egypt, ancient Atlantis—you pick a universe, a cosmos, it doesn't matter—there's always something going on. There is always somebody on your case. Dogs have fleas; people have each other. We're born to die. Life is a continuing tragedy, tragicomedy. Everything and everyone we love suffers. We suffer. How can you be happy? Life is a horror show, isn't it? Well, sure, certainly, I mean, yeah, obviously. Anybody who doesn't see that has not grown up and known life.

Spiritual balance is the ability to—in spite of all that—remain happy. Not to be hostile to your neighbor when they're being hostile, not to get caught up in the trivia. Spiritual balance, in other words, is the ability to climb up the mountain and be in a world of light. The lack of spiritual balance is to get so hassled by the details of life and trying to get everything so straight to climb up the spiritual mountain that you never really do.

You wanted to have a great run today. But there were so many things you had to do first, and running is your favorite thing—it's when you feel best, your body's alive, your mind is awake, everything's great. You had to make the bed, you had to meditate, you had to work, you had to clean. And by the time it came, your moment for running came, you were so tired that you didn't run. That's the lack of spiritual balance.

Spiritual balance is the ability to get above it all, to see that there's something more noble—call it divine, happy, bright, brilliant—to this thing we call life. Spiritual balance is the ability to be straight with yourself. The purpose of life is happiness. What else could it possibly be? The purpose of life is something that, of course, that we choose. Life doesn't have a purpose. Don't be absurd. The cosmos just is. But by choosing a purpose, in yoga, in Buddhism, we learn that by choosing a purpose, we choose an outcome. Our purpose, our intent, is the outcome immediately. If you feel that the purpose of life is happiness, enlightenment, understanding, then that's what you'll experience. If you feel the purpose of life is struggle, Darwinian fitness, you know, dog eat dog, then I guess you'll be eaten by a dog, I don't know what will happen. Or you'll eat a dog. You experience or you become what you focus on—this is one of the principle rules in yoga.

Balance is to choose happiness, to feel that the purpose of life is to love—not necessarily to be loved—to be happy, to be conscious, to be aware, to be fulfilled. And if that's what you seek, that's what you'll find. Yoga and Buddhism are simply a methodology, a way of becoming one with the part of us, with the part of ourselves, that is happy. There are other parts of us. There are parts of us that are miserable. There are parts that don't care. There are parts that hate. There are parts that love. There are parts that are cruel. There are parts that are kind. There are parts that are reasonable. There are parts that are unreasonable. You know, you live inside your mind. Who are you kidding? You're not fooling anybody. You know what's going on inside your mind. Everything—everything. The more moral you pretend to be, the less moral you are. The less moral you try to be, the more moral you are. You know how it is. We all do. We all live in it.

And everybody's experience is about the same. Frustrating. Sometimes happy. But some people have found a secret to living, a secret to happiness. They practice yoga and Buddhism, esoteric Buddhism, esoteric yoga. Not just going to the temple and being there at a ceremony and dressing up. That's the church Buddhism. Real esoteric Buddhism, real yoga, is to move beyond this world. It involves the use of the mind—to take the mind from the plane of the earth and transpose it into planes of pure and perfect happiness, to transpose your awareness field beyond this life, beyond this moment, into the planes of light.

The planes of light exist, just as the earth exists, just as the oceans exist, just as the ages exist, the planes of light exist. They are just beyond this dimension, just a little way down the street. Yoga is a method of unifying the energies of the body, the mind and the spirit and directing them towards infinity, towards the planes of light, towards the one perfect creation that is inside your own mind.

The planes of light are inside your mind. Infinity is inside your mind. Eternity is inside your mind. Happiness, the Grinch—everything is inside the mind, all heavens and hells and anything in between or outside of them. Nirvana is inside the mind—not the brain, not the cell structures—the mind. The intelligence principle, *bodhi*, consciousness, awareness, that which we are, that which we seek to be—everything is inside the mind. The question is, where is it? How do you get there? Will it fulfill you? Is there a greater ecstasy, a greater happiness?

Balance, spiritual balance, is the principle that allows the mind to be still. You can't expect the world to settle down, everything to work out, in order for you to practice meditation and to be happy. If you are waiting for the perfect person, the perfect meditation, the perfect day, there's no such thing. You're the perfect person. This is the perfect day and this is the perfect meditation. Life is what you make it. But you have to do something. You have to get control of the mind. You've got to get your power up and do something and not just sit around.

As Dr. Seuss says, "You can't just be sitting in that waiting room." Everybody in the waiting room of life in *Oh, the Places You'll Go*, in his final, if not final books. Everybody is waiting, waiting, waiting, waiting, waiting. Waiting for everything. You've got to go do things. Yoga is not a waiting. It's a doing, today. And balance is the hardest part. Of all the things in yoga, all the things in Buddhism, self-discovery and the enlightenment cycle, balance is the most difficult thing because it's overlooked. It's not intrinsically the hardest thing. It's no harder than anything else. But because it's underestimated, because we don't really consider it deeply enough, it's overlooked. That's why it's life's hardest thing. We think, in other words, that it is not important to be balanced.

In martial arts, one of the first things that you learn, one of the most important things, is to be balanced. If you're not balanced, anybody can knock you over. If you're balanced, then you're in pretty good shape. You know you can defend yourself.

Balance is a central principle in all building, in architecture and design. If a thing isn't balanced, it falls apart. It falls over. It's a principle. It's a way of trying to talk about being at the center of things, to use that word. To be balanced is to be happy. When you're happy, you are the center of things. When you're happy, it's pretty tough to knock you over. You can handle whatever comes along in life. You can handle the bright days, the dark days and the intermediate days.

Happiness is found, then, principally in meditation. When the eyes are closed, when the mind is still, when you're fixed on a chakra and you go through that magical doorway into the inner world where everything is still and beautiful and perfect, and let your mind relax and flow out into eternity, into light, into brightness, into happiness, it's there. But you have to connect with it. You have to exert some effort. Then you'll notice a subtle smile will form on your face; a lightness will fill your being, a brightness.

All the fake, dull thoughts that you think, all the ridiculous philosophies, the necessities, all the things that won't matter a bit when you're dead, but boy, do they seem to be overpoweringly important when you're alive—these things fade away for a while, for a few minutes. For a while the heaviness, the awesome responsibility of being human goes away. And you get to play in fields of light. You get to play in eternity, in the brightness. And that brightness is powerful. It's not simply a transient happiness that you experience in meditation which creates balance. It's a transformative light. Light transforms—inner light—very powerful. The inner light is the most powerful thing there is.

You know, sometimes it's hard to see something in human life. I mean, we see what we see. If the fog rolls in, we can't see anything. If it's there for a while, we forget that there's anything to see in that wall of fog. A couple hundred yards away is the perimeter of our vision, and the mind automatically adjusts and we forget that there's anything else. We deal with what we can see between here and the bank of fog. I'm sitting here looking at a bank of fog and wondering whether I can get increased interest on my checking account there. I don't know.

Along the bay the speedboats are passing by and the fog's rolling in. And a little while ago I could see for several miles, when I just started this tape. But now I can only see a few hundred yards. That's what we call *maya*, illusion, symbolically represented. The fog prevents us from seeing what's right there, and we forget about it.

Most people get so caught up in life that they forget that the purpose of life is to be happy, that happiness is something that is wonderful. They spend so much time trying to be happy that when it's time to be happy, they just forget. It just rolls away. There's nothing anybody can do about it except that person. Nobody can make you happy but yourself. Things occupy us, people occupy us, but they don't make us happy if we're honest. What makes us happy is to have a spiritual experience, to experience spirit, something not so gross as all this matter around us. Matter is fun for a while, but ultimately, it's the spiritual experience, the ecstatic transcendence, where we leap—beyond what we know and call the world—into the eternal light where nothing is for sure, nothing is certain, that experience of ecstasy in the deepest meditation. That's happiness or whatever you want to call it—peace, stillness, something beyond the transient frustrations. The pain of the body, the despair and disillusionment of the mind, the sorrow of the heart—beyond all that nonsense, there's brightness.

Yoga is fulfillment—sitting, meditating, leading a compact, fun, bright, tight life, blowing your ego out the door and your self-importance, letting go of the things that hurt you, as they hurt you, holding onto things that are happy. When they change and they start to hurt you, you let them go. But I mean, what else would be intelligent? What else can you do?

You love someone, and you love them because it's happy and then suddenly you're unhappy loving them. What do you do? You get burned. You stop loving? Well, no, if you stop loving them, you just move the love someplace else. If you've got your money in the bank, and the bank's credit rating drops and it's a problem, you don't give up banking. You just move your money to a bank that's better.

Love has very little to do with a person. It comes from us. You can love a surprisingly great number of people. They just have to fit the right parameters. Love comes from ourselves, not from someone else. You can love infinity, eternity, Scottie dogs, sports, work, play, the feelings of being alive, the earth, the sky, the fire, the wind, fancy cars, swimming pools, challenging experiences, technological understandings. There's a lot you can love. To love is to be balanced, to extend one's self beyond just the sense of self, of what matters to me today, of what I think is going to please me, of avoiding what I think is unhappy. That's balance. That's happiness.

If you become obsessive in your spiritual practice, if you just try and try and try and try, and you push and push, you're not going to be happy. You're going to be obsessive. If you try and make everything work out perfectly, try and just make everything come together the way you want to, once in a while that'll happen. That will be pretty, but sometimes it's nice when it doesn't. Sometimes it's nice when unexpected things happen. What is perfection anyway, in the physical? It's an idea that we have. And when it doesn't happen that way, we get all bent out of shape and frustrated and angry and then unhappy, and we take it out on everybody else, including ourselves.

On the other hand—there are five fingers—on the other hand, the possibilities of perfection, beyond the conception of limited order that an individual might have, the possibilities are greater. Take chaotic mathematics, for example. The universe is chaos, I guess. You could see it as chaos, but chaos is wimping out. It's wimp talk. It's sniveling. Snivelers say that there is chaos, friends. There's no chaos. There are just people who don't understand what's out there, and they have a label for it, and they don't want to deal with it, so we'll call it chaos when it gets over their chip size. There's no chaos. There are just different levels of order in the universe. Chaos, chaotic mathematics, is essentially the study of chaos, that is to say it can't be chaos if you can study it and it has an order. There are just different types of order.

Don't be a sniveler. Don't say you can't be happy, you can't be enlightened. How do you know? "It's all chaotic. Nothing ever works out." Sure, all kinds of things work out every day, and then they dissolve and it's another day. There's growth, maturation. Watch a plant grow. Tell me things don't work out. All those cells working together, striving toward the light, putting out new buds, new leaves. Life's a miracle—all that RNA at work. Life's a miracle, miraculous. We're miracles. So don't deny yourself the possibility of the miracle of happiness, because then you'll be balanced. You can approach anything and everything, or nothing, and all will be well.

I've been teaching yoga for a while, and Buddhism, many, many, many lifetimes. I've had lots of students, disciples. A long time ago, many lives ago, I had great teachers, radical, radically wonderful teachers who brought me through the enlightenment cycle like I'm bringing some people through the enlightenment cycle in this and other lives. And the thing that I've noticed, that I learned from my own teachers a long time ago in another universe, the thing that I've observed in the successful students that I've had over the lifetimes, is a quality which I think you can develop. I think it's something that's in each of us, and it's a quality of gentleness but strength, silliness but maturity, optimism but a sense that it's not going to be easy, if not impossibly difficult, but we're going to get it done anyway, a kind of quiet fortitude which is renewed by a person's love of light.

People come and people go in spiritual practice, like in anything. And then there are those who stay and grow and really make it, really develop, really become transcendentally happy and ecstatic, bright beyond conception. The ones who do that, I think, have a love of light that they allow to develop. I think most people are chicken, snivelers, and like we say in East L.A., "Snivelers, man! They're snivelers!" They're afraid, afraid to experience their brighter side.

You have to be courageous in life to allow a lightness to engage your being. It's easy to be a jerk. You know, just look at the world—meaning, to be unhappy when you have so much to be happy about, that's what I call a jerk. When you're given this human body in this weird, interesting world, the possibilities of exploring so many things, not just yoga and Buddhism but there are so many interesting things to get your mind and body into and your spirit into. To be unhappy with all this weird stuff around us just seems to me to be such a waste—that's a jerk.

Intelligence, on the other hand, is the apprehension of the newness of each moment and being creative, not just sitting there and if there's nothing good on TV being frustrated, but shutting the thing off, disconnecting it, you know? And going and taking up kayaking or cross-country skiing or something. Do something. Don't be in the waiting room—waiting, waiting, waiting for the perfect person, the perfect career, the perfect meditation teacher, whatever it is. Just go do something, something fun, something bright. Learn something. Be a student of life.

But if you're a sniveler, a whiner, a complainer, you'll never be happy. We all have that side, but we get it under control. Get a little stoical and just, you know, take the pain. But then turn your attention with your will. Study the great teachings of the teachers, read books that expand you, that are bright. See films, plays, art forms that elevate your consciousness, that bring you into a sense of how beautiful this world is, how beautiful other worlds are, how beautiful nirvana—the transcendental—is.

You know, chill out. Life is hard work no matter what you do. There is always going to be pain. There is always going to be pleasure. But what is not always going to be there is balance, happiness. That's a personal decision.

That's what I'm trying to tell you, my young friends. To be happy is not something that happens to you because you're born and you live on this earth. Nor is it something that happens to you because you're rich. I have a lot of, you know, wealthy students. They're not necessarily happy. I know a lot of wealthy people in West Los Angeles. They're not necessarily happy. And in other places. Money doesn't make you happy. You might as well have some if you can, but that's not the ticket. Health is nice. It doesn't make you happy. You only notice it if it's not there. Fame doesn't make you happy. It just makes you look in the mirror a lot, worry about how you look today for your audience. They are fun things to pursue if you get a kick out of them, but what makes you happy is not being born, it's not having a human body, it's not this world. It's a decision. It's a decision that you make every day, and that you renew, that you strengthen.

You decide to be happy. You find out how. You find the happiest person you know, but not happy in a facile sense. We're not talking Rodney Dangerfield who makes me laugh, but I have no idea if he's personally happy. You find a special teacher, someone who doesn't just look majestic and say the right words, but someone who themselves is obviously intrinsically happy in a very deep and quiet way. Someone humorous, someone you can see if you probe their depth beyond just the external caretaker personality they may choose to manifest, someone who is really at peace with themselves. They've got it wired. You learn happiness from someone who knows it, like you learn mathematics from someone who knows it.

It's a way of being. It's a conscious decision, and the shortcut to happiness, spiritual balance, is to meditate. If you meditate twice a day and not just sit there but actually meditate, raise your attention with your willpower to a brighter sphere of consciousness, learn the discipline of meditation and practice it in, hopefully, a very beautiful way—if you do that, and you have a teacher to direct you who is happy, not just someone who has good PR, then you will find happiness. But it doesn't just come. Otherwise everyone would be happy in the world. Hardly anybody's happy, for a moment. Take a walk today and look at how many people smile. Not many. Look at how troubled they are. Look at how unhappy, how stressed out. Whether we go through the ghetto or we go through Beverly Hills, they're stressed out. They're not happy out there.

And even the ones who are happy, what they call happiness, are just looking at the fog bank. And they can see a hundred yards and that's all. Real happiness is something most people never know. What we experience in yoga, in deep meditation, that ecstasy is beyond what human beings call happiness. Yet it's human beings who experience it, who practice yoga.

If you're interested in happiness, if you want to be balanced in life, if you want to be able to handle death and life, success and failure, then I would suggest that you practice yoga and Buddhism, not just go through the motions, not just do what everybody else does. But that you find a teacher who is happy, focus your life on happy and beautiful things, put a smile on your face even if you don't feel like it.

Don't just sit there. Go do something. And don't expect that it's going to be fun unless you make it fun.

You've got to work on things. That's when you're happy. Work on things not just with obsession but with a smile, with a sense of brightness. There's pain in any endeavor. Happiness doesn't just mean, you know, everything works out. Usually nothing works out, but you get a kick out of it anyway. It's fun to push it sometimes, to use your will to see how far you can get in life. In college and high school, you get A's. That's the game you play. If you don't play that game, you're missing all the fun. How many can you get? In the human world, it's how much money can you make? If you miss that, you are missing the fun.

There are ways to creatively use your will. When you sit down to meditate, it's how high can you get, how bright can you be? When you work out, it's how clean a workout can you do, not pushing so hard that you hurt your body and you can't work out the next day, but within that parameter, how hard can you push it? When it's relaxing, it's to relax completely and let go. When it's loving, it's to love completely and then move your love around, of course, if you get hurt. Change S and L's.

Balance is wisdom. Balance is the ability to be happy in the midst of the most chaotic or even boring or transient circumstances of any type. Put a smile on your face. Do it.

Don't sit in the waiting room of life. Go do something, happily. Hopefully, it will involve meditation and yoga and Buddhism.

CHAPTER FIVE

WISDOM

Wisdom is the ability to do two things at once—to be in the world and of it, and enjoy it and participate in it fully and successfully and, at the same time, to not be here at all, to be in realms of light, to be in the super-conscious state, to be in samadhi, beyond all this. That's true wisdom.

Wisdom is the ability to take care of your life properly, to know what's right for you, to have assessed what is the right path and to follow it with heart, with your full spirit and your full mind and your full body—to not have reservations. When you do something half-heartedly, you don't get much of a result. When you do it fully, you get a great result.

Wisdom is the ability to let go. Children are wise in a funny kind of a way. Perhaps their interests aren't as vested; they haven't developed as many vested interests of self. They can just kind of let go. They can move from one neighborhood to another, one school to another fairly easily. As they get older, it becomes more difficult. There's a wisdom, a lack of self-consciousness, that is innocence. I think innocence is the greatest wisdom.

85

To be wise doesn't always mean to have a wrinkled face and sparkly eyes. Usually it does. To be wise means to be still inside, to see the motions of eternity in day-to-day life and beyond this. True wisdom is freedom. True wisdom is enlightenment. At the same time, wisdom has a practical side—the ability to make good choices. The best choice anyone can make is to educate themselves. You can't be too educated. It's like, you know, in Beverly Hills—they say you can't be too thin or too rich. Well, in the world of wisdom, you can't be too wise.

Wisdom is something that seeks itself. The wiser you become, the more you realize that you'd like to know what there is to know. There's worldly wisdom—the wisdom of success, the wisdom of achievement, how to deal with things, politics, a political sense about life. To be sharp, to be clear, to be focused, not showing all your cards, not letting anyone really know who you are or what you're like—there's a wisdom to this. Why should anyone know? It's personal. It's private, who you are. And also, if you define yourself, then you're defined. People have a fixed impression of you. They hold you in their mind a certain way, and that actually makes it difficult to change.

It's very wise to be inaccessible—not to hide, but simply not to be too personal. Keep the deepest feelings of your heart to yourself. They tend to stay more pure if you do. There is a wisdom to that.

Wisdom is knowing that if you bend, you don't have to break. Sometimes it's necessary to go with the flow of life, to let life dictate experience and not necessarily allow ourselves to dictate it. In other words, let's say you wanted to build a house, and you went to a place and you had your idea of what a house should be like there, and you built that house. That's not wisdom. That's your idea of a house. Wisdom would suggest that we go to a place and feel the place—feel its presence and feel its absence. Determine if the house should be built there at all by the feelings there. What is it that the place wants? And then allow the formation of the house—the kind of house—to come through us, to allow it to be drawn out of us by the place. That's wisdom.

In other words, in the West, the wise are usually thought of as leaders. In the Far East, the wise are very often thought of as followers. It's a different sensibility. Wisdom here means that you're the boss, you're the top gun, you're the hot shot. And that's a type of wisdom, certainly. But there's another wisdom, and that's the wisdom of following—the wisdom of not taking the lead with your ego, but allowing yourself to be still, to reflect, to meditate, to be conscious, and seeing that there are templates in life that will guide you.

There are templates in the universe that you can follow. Most people can't see them. They're sort of like pointers. They are there, and they will show you what to do and what not to do. But in order to see them, you have to make your mind very quiet, very still. You have to be somewhat serene and balanced, happy with your life, with who you are and how you're doing. Because if your spirit is in a state of confusion, if you're restless emotionally, if you're unhappy, if you just can't settle down, then you can't really see very much other than your restlessness. If the lake is all stirred up and there are a lot of waves, you can't see below the waves. It's agitated. It's muddy. If you allow the lake to become calm, if we wait until it becomes still, the mud settles. The waves stop and we can see all the way into its depths and know what's going on down there.

Love is a kind of wisdom. There's a wisdom to loving. Love is sometimes pleasurable, sometimes painful, sometimes ecstatic. But there's a wisdom; there's a knowing that comes from loving. I think it's a mistake not to love. I think some people think that spiritual practice means to divorce themselves from love and all other emotions. I don't think so. I think one just must love more deeply and without the sense of that which you love being your personal possession.

Love makes you wise. Pain doesn't necessarily make you wise—it just makes you wary. But love means to communicate, to commune, to be part of something. Love unites. Pain divides. Hate divides even more. Hate separates and brings us down to a very physical plane. Love elevates us to a plane of spirit.

I think if you are truly wise, you love life very deeply. You love your life, the things in your life, transient though they may be, you love them—the moments, the feelings of being alive, the feeling of the morning, the afternoon, the evening, nighttime, the wind and the way it feels, the color of the rocks, the earth, the sounds of the city, the sounds and feelings of the peoples. There is something to this fabric of life that's beautiful, and I think if you find the world simply unpleasant, I don't think that's a sign of wisdom. I think that's a sign of a lack of wisdom.

Certainly there are places you don't want to be because it doesn't work for you. There are things that you'd find draining or not elevating. But to not see the beauty, the romance in the universe—in other words, just because it doesn't work for you doesn't mean that it's not wonderful for someone else. Wisdom is the ability, I think, to realize that everyone has their own *dharma,* that everyone goes their own way. And your way and what works for you is not the ultimate good. It might be the ultimate good for you today. To be flexible and know that other people have different ways, and maybe you even have different ways that you haven't discovered, that tomorrow you can let go of how you have to do things and who you are and how you have to be—that, to me, is wisdom—to be flexible, to be lucid.

Wisdom has to do with how you live, with how you conduct yourself, commerce, with how you deal with people and things, certainly. And in the Orient, there is a wisdom that suggests that it's good not always to be too demonstrative. In other words, in Buddhism we have a great deal of etiquette. Etiquette is an intelligent way to live. Etiquette is simply ways of living that have been practiced that conserve energy, that create a more pleasant life. Etiquette is not seen as something false or unnecessary. It allows people to live together in harmony. It allows people to live in harmony with their environment. And when we lack etiquette, we trash things. We trash each other. We trash our environment. We lose sight of the value of things. And then, of course, we suffer. We suffer the alienation that has to follow when our spirit is disconnected from our physical awareness.

Etiquette is an intelligent way to live. In other words, in Buddhism, in spiritual practice, Taoism, different forms of mystical philosophy be they East or West, there are certain principles and practices, ways of living, that you will learn from reading and from being around advanced students and mostly just from your teacher. These are methods that have been handed down for thousands of years that are tried and true, tested and occasionally changed as civilization or society or life changes. And that's the outer form of Buddhism. The outer form of Buddhism, of practice, is etiquette—a series of ways to live intelligently that keep you alive, awake and happy, wakeful.

The wisdom of *samadhi* is quite different. That's the undifferentiated experience of reality. In other words, wisdom—if it's really a higher level wisdom—can't be written down. It can't be spoken. I can't tell you what it is. True wisdom is the knowledge of the universe that is beyond any physical expression. Music, perhaps, expresses it better than words. It can put us more in touch with it, certain types of music, art. But real wisdom is samadhi—to sit in meditation, to stop thought, to go beyond all things into the clear light of reality in which there is no time, nor space, nor dimensionality.

That's samadhi—perfect absorption to the point where there is no sense of being absorbed—full consciousness, but not the consciousness of the body, not the consciousness of the world, not the consciousness of daily life, not the consciousness of knowing that you are having an experience.

If you're meditating and you sense that you are in ecstasy, that's not really samadhi. If you sense ecstasy, that's not really samadhi. Samadhi is beyond those things. Samadhi means that you have become the light, for a time, and there is no sense of an experiencer. There is no sense that, while I'm sitting here and even though I'm not thinking, I'm having an experience—I'm experiencing ecstasy, I'm experiencing wisdom, knowledge or something profound. Real samadhi is off the game board, friends. It's not something that you are even aware of. And you might say, well, how do you know you were in samadhi? You know. Things don't have to be logical. You know. You know when your awareness returns to the plane of self and ideation that you've been beyond it. There's a knowing. And that's enough.

Real wisdom, the deepest spiritual wisdom, does not occur here—it can't. Here being in this body and in this mind and in this physical universe. Real wisdom is something that you have to move into the planes of the highest light to experience. And you can't bring yourself with you. You have to go to the other side. The other side is what is beyond the mind's knowing.

There's the world of the physical. There's the astral, the

dimensions, the dimensional planes that you can traverse in your astral body. There are the planes of light, which are referred to as the causal, and you experience in your causal body. Those are the meditative planes and dimensions, the planes of light, but that's still something that you can reference. Even the planes of light, while the experience in the higher planes of light is certainly a kind of samadhi—salvikalpa samadhi—nirvikalpa samadhi is to go to the other side, to experience the other side.

As I said before, the other side is beyond knowing. You cannot know what you experience on the other side, here. It cannot be known. The chip size here is too limited. You can't grasp your own experience. That's the true wisdom. True wisdom is on the other side of this life. Not in death, but beyond the grasp of the conscious mind. That's where real wisdom lies. Someone who is truly wise makes that journey many times a day. They go back and forth from this world to the other side, and when you come back, you don't remember the journey, but yet you are the journey. Perhaps it's more apparent to someone else even than it is to you because the you that was you before you went to the other side is never the same when you come back—going to the other side of consciousness and to, in other words, nirvana.

Nirvana is the other side, the source of all things, where all the aggregates come from, where the templates of infinity are. To go to the other side, or where they come from, anyway, is wisdom. Wisdom is getting there. Wisdom is nirvana, and it's something that can't be known here. I know it seems incongruous, but it's only incongruous from this perspective, from the perspective of the dialectical consciousness of division, of time and space.

In your meditation, you're seeking not simply to experience ecstasy or the planes of light—that's a type of wisdom. You're not only gaining power and clarity of mind to lead a better physical life, to be healthy, happy, to be spiritual, to be successful, to be compassionate—those are types of wisdom. But the real wisdom, the higher wisdom, is to go to the other side, to go to nirvana, to be that. That's the ultimate wisdom—not that it's ultimate in the sense that it's a final stage. There is no final stage in nirvana. Nirvana is beyond definition. It is not quantifiable.

One goes to the other side and—returns. You climb to the top of the mountain. Let's say you go to the Himalayas and you're drawn to tops of mountains. You climb way up through the ice and the snow and you get to the top of K2 or Mount Everest or mountains that perhaps are not as well known. You get up there. You stand there and you see the ranges, of the mountains, the Himalayas spread out at your feet. And it's different there. There's a different feeling there. There's a different awareness there. It vibrates very fast. The mountains themselves and the dimensions that are associated with those mountains vibrate very quickly. You are up there in the realm of the eternal snows, and then you come back down.

And then when you're down here, you sort of forget about what happened up there, what those experiences and feelings were like. You go back to life and your house and your job and what you do. But it changes you. It clarifies your purpose. It makes life more abundant to have had that experience. It's not transient. It's eternal. You touch eternality at the top of the Himalayas.

Well, samadhi is the top of the Himalayas in spiritual practice. Nirvikalpa samadhi or sahaja samadhi—that's all the way up. You get up above the cloud line to the land of eternal snows, and it's ecstasy, beyond ecstasy. Then you come back. Some people say, "Why do you come back?" Well you don't, exactly. I mean the journey changes you so much that it's not exactly the same you. Life reorders you when you go into the clear light. Even the causal structure is liquefied. In the clear light of reality, in the *dharmakaya,* in that highest, purest formation that is existence, it changes us into beings of light. We come back and we're kind of ordinary. You know, you're still walking around. And you still have to eat and live and exist. But it changes your experience of those things. You're less here, and a part of you is still on the other side. The more you journey there, well, after a while, you're always on the other side and always here, and that's what we call sahaja samadhi. It's not a journey like nirvikalpa.

Nirvikalpa samadhi means you're sitting in meditation and you go beyond just the planes of light to nirvana, total absorption in nirvana, in complete perfection, and there is no sense, of course, of that—it's all on the other side. But then, you're sitting in meditation, then you come back, the eyes open and gradually you go back through the planes of light and here you are, back in the saddle again.

Sahaja samadhi—you've just gone back and forth so many times that there's no back and forth for you. All you see is enlightenment and this world and the other side. Well, there's no other side anymore. You're in a condition of perpetual wakefulness. Which doesn't mean, by the way, that you know everything. It means that you're wakeful. It doesn't mean that you have all physical knowledge. Some people think that enlightenment means that you know everything. It means that you can speak all languages, that you can fix cars if you need to, all kinds of stuff, things that you haven't studied come to you—not necessarily at all. That's a storybook, Hollywood-ized, version of the enlightenment experience.

Enlightenment has nothing to do with physical knowledge. It's the knowledge, the higher knowledge—maybe that's not even the right word—the experience of existence. Existence is infinite. There are countless universes and creations taking place simultaneously, all times present and past. The far-flung universes exist forever, and all manner of beings and creations are there. Everything that can be and everything that can't be exists somewhere. It's beyond the mind's ability to grasp. And, certainly nirvana means seeing and knowing that vastness. But beyond the far-flung infinities there's something else. Beyond the planes of light there's something else—that isn't a broad-based knowing, that isn't the sense of a person perceiving what knowledge is, what wisdom is. That's nirvana. It's a word that's used to describe the other side.

Somewhere there's an essence. It's not a physical somewhere. But there's an essence for all of this. There, there's nothing but light, but not even in a temporal, spatial sense. It just is. And there, there is no time, no space, no self. Existence just is perfect. There's no sense of this world, of time and space. That's nirvana. It's the center of things. Then there are the outer bandings of attention. In other words, the universe is a mind, and at the center of its mind is nirvana—center not so much in a spatial sense—that's nirvana. Nirvana is the pure and perfect *suchness* or *thatness* of being. Then, outside of nirvana, the planes begin—the subtlest planes that vibrate the fastest, the planes of light, all the way on down through the astral realms through the physical and so on.

Life is perception, and we perceive through different parts of the body of the universe. But nirvana has nothing to do with any of this. None of this is there—who you are, what you are, your pain, your pleasure, your life, your death, this world, all these myriad beings we see before us. They're not in nirvana. Nor can you say that it's light. And you can't journey there and have experiences. You can't know what's there because *you* can't be there. There is no "you" there.

The journey to the other side means the loss of the self, at least temporarily, because it just weighs too much to go there. It's too much baggage. Nirvana is that perpetual knowingness of the universe and its perfection. And then there's all this—this abstraction, this life we lead, this play of war and peace and pleasure and pain and birth and growth and maturation and decay and death—the thing we call life and all beings call life, that's so different from nirvana, yet it comes from it. How strange.

Wisdom is to see the difference between nirvana and this—this world, this self-reflection that the mind creates. To do that, obviously you have to know nirvana, to get to the other side. But wisdom is also to see that there's no difference at all between nirvana and here, between *samsara* and *nirvana*. There's only one seamless, perfect reality. Wisdom isn't to know these words. Wisdom isn't to have ideas or philosophies. Those are just thoughts. Wisdom is to be that—to be that perfect consciousness. That's the greatest wisdom there is.

And then it's good to know that you go on green, you slow down on yellow and you stop on red. The wisdom of enlightenment does not preclude practicality. Some people seem to think that wisdom does, and that if you're enlightened somehow you are not in touch with life and the pulse of the physical. Au contraire. The more enlightened you are, the more basic you are. The higher you go, the deeper you become, and the more conscious you are of the physical and the sensorial.

The pure and perfect radiant light that you experience in the planes of light and the experience of going to the other side to nirvana clarifies and simplifies your view of all things, and you see the world with greater clarity, because it's not obscured by personal desire, vanity, egotism and thought, by illusions. Human beings have illusions. The enlightened don't have illusions, they just see things as they are, and in that seeing, they see ecstasy and joy. They see the play of life.

Knowledge is, as I said, many things—the ability to love, the ability to feel, the ability to probe the depths and the heights of life. It's the experience of the experiencer, and at the same time, it's beyond that. So many types of knowledge, so much to explore. You know, so much enlightenment, so much time.

On your journey, try to remember that there is no end. That's true knowledge. There is no final knowledge. There is no final enlightenment. That's a very finite, human way of looking at things. It is a categorization that implies a hierarchical way of seeing things. Life is really relational, not hierarchical. Hierarchical is a human way of looking at things. Relational is much more the way things are. Things are relational. They depend upon each other. They influence each other. Everything is connected. Hierarchies are mental schemes. They usually involve good and bad, good and evil, better and worse, before and after, here and there and everywhere. And those are convenient ways to talk about things and to negotiate the physical world and sometimes the astral worlds to get through the day. But life is really relational.

True wisdom is to see and understand your relationship with the universe, with God, with infinity, and with all things both finite and infinite. When you gain that relational knowledge, then you're wise. Then you're more careful. Then you're more kind because you see that there is no reason not to be. There's no reason not to love. There's no reason not to be joyous. There's no reason not to celebrate because all of this means nothing—absolutely nothing. Why not be happy? Why not be free? Why not endeavor? It's a happier way to be. If you're truly wise, then you reflect the universe and you're relational in your approach to things. You're a mirror of infinity. That's wisdom.

CHAPTER SIX

ENLIGHTENMENT

Enlightenment is the complete awareness of life without mental modifications. Enlightenment is the state of awareness we reach when our consciousness is one with infinity, with the infinite consciousness of life itself. Enlightenment is not a state of mind, although all states of mind are contained within it. It is the best of all things, the brightest of all lights. It is union with immortality, timelessness, and with the temporal, with all the myriad worlds, planes and things that simply can't be put into words.

Enlightenment exists within everything. There is nothing that can be separate from enlightenment. But when I talk about enlightenment, when I discuss it with my students, I am referring to an experience, a journey—the journey to light. Enlightenment in this sense is a journey into cosmic consciousness—to be completely aware of eternity, to be aware not just of this moment or this world, but of timelessness, of space, of organic life and what lies beyond it.

Think of enlightenment as a journey. Today you woke up and anything can happen. You could live any type of life. You could be rich. You could be poor. You could be wise. You could be ignorant. It doesn't really matter because no matter what happens, there is enlightenment. All the things you see that threaten you and make you afraid, all the things that you see that attract you, the things that you're indifferent to or perhaps don't even know about—they don't really matter. Life is like a dream. It's transient. For one moment, we're in the stream of life. We're awake. We're having experiences. Then we're asleep. It's all washed away; at best it becomes a memory that fades. Death is a sleep and life is an awakening. And in each lifetime, we awaken to a different condition.

The wakefulness, the state of wakefulness that I refer to, that enlightened teachers refer to, is a condition of ecstasy, a condition of tremendous beauty, a permanent state of wakefulness that defies sleep. Sleep is dreams of another kind. Death—the experiences in the after-death plane, between lifetimes, between incarnations—is a different kind of dream which we forget upon waking to this life and this world.

Enlightenment is a journey, a journey into light, a journey into self-knowledge, a journey into beauty, reflection, awareness. The infinitude of being calls us to become conscious of itself. Now this might sound like a lot of euphoria to some. It might sound just like a lot of words, a rhapsody of words that don't necessarily connect and aren't practical. That is certainly not the case. To be conscious, to be aware of what you are aware of, is not something that you can defend or express. It simply is.

Yes, there's the surface of life. There are the day-to-day activities of human beings, plants, animals, astral beings—the endless movements of creation. And then there's nirvana. Nirvana is absolute ecstasy, absolute stillness, a presence—to be in the center of the mind of God, to be completely conscious, forever, of forever, to be in the timeless, misty realm, the nexus of all things. All universes, all intelligences, all cycles of being, come from it. And they go back to it. It sustains them; it holds them here. That's the world of enlightenment. The day-to-day life we lead has nothing to do with enlightenment. We're unaware of it. It's just around the corner, and we don't see it. It's in front of us, and we don't see it. We are it, and we don't see it.

Enlightenment is happiness—happiness in the most profound and yet most simple sense. Enlightenment is, as I said before, a journey—a journey into cosmic consciousness. And meditation is the key to enlightenment. To meditate, to make your mind still and supremely aware, to penetrate the void, the essence, the substance, and go beyond both to what is referred to as the clear light of reality—clear in the sense that it doesn't have a definite color; light in the sense that it's not solid, yet it is, pure energy; reality in the sense that it is that which is most real, that which is actual, meaning it doesn't change. It's always here.

The pathway to enlightenment is your life. Each being is walking along that pathway, having experiences, gaining knowledge, learning by doing. What else is there to do? And their progression is beyond judgment. It just is. But then there's the study of enlightenment. In other words, life is enlightenment, the great process of life, and we can say that everybody's on their way to enlightenment or they all are enlightenment—and from a certain perspective that's true. But then there's the experience of enlightenment—to yoke your consciousness, to join yourself to immortality, to—in this very life—be very aware of what lies beyond the boundaries of cognitive perception, beyond the boundaries of thought, reflection and self-awareness as seen through the personality.

Why become enlightened? You know, why join the military? Why get married? Why cross the ocean? Why stay at home? Why stay single? Why avoid the army? It's a personal choice. There's something in a person that draws them to the light. It's karma, ultimately. Karma is not a cop out. The word, as it's frequently used, is a cop out. If you say something is your "karma," that seems to free us from responsibility. If you say, "Well, this happened to me. I was born into this life, in this condition, or these things just happened to me because it's my karma," it's as if you have nothing to do with it. Certainly there is chance. But that isn't really the esoteric meaning of karma. The esoteric meaning of karma is that you are who you are, and you experience what you experience because of what you've done and what you've been.

Your karma is who you are today. Your karma is the sum total of your awareness field. Your awareness field is comprised of all the experiences that you've had in this life and all other lives. In this incarnation, you are born into the world with a certain karma. That is to say, at the moment of birth, you had a certain facility. One is potential, and one is immediately available. The karma of immediate availability is the wakefulness, the condition of your awareness field when you're born. The karma of potentiality is what's stored inside you from your past lives.

Just as you are today the experience and the product of everything that you've known and gone through in this lifetime, so, at the moment of birth you are the product of everything that's occurred to you in every lifetime that you've had. But like an inheritance that you don't come into until you're perhaps 21, when you're born you don't necessarily have at your fingertips, at your control, everything that you are, everything that you've been in your past lives.

In the enlightenment cycle, attention is paid to bringing back the awareness field, the total you, from other lives. This does not simply mean the memory of experience past—that may or may not be helpful—but rather to draw on the internal power and intelligence, the knowledge, the wisdom that you've amassed in other lifetimes. And if you have amassed any *siddha* powers, to bring them back also because they can be quite useful on the journey to enlightenment. So to do this, meditation is the key that unlocks or opens the door. Meditation will bring back the powers and awareness of the past. And even more immediately, it'll expand your consciousness today to places you've never been, to experiences that you've never had.

Meditation is the pathway to enlightenment. Meditation is to stop thought, to silence the mind, to move the ego aside and to simply be still, open, clear, bright and fully conscious. Meditation is not an active movement in a sense, not in its deeper sense. There is a sense of activity in the beginning of meditation. The shuttle astronauts are going into space. They have to blast off and there is a great amount of energy expended to get up into orbit or to get beyond the gravitational pull of the earth. Once they have done that, they shut the engines off. There's no gravity, or they've achieved the orbit they desire and they simply coast. Then space will move them.

In meditation, in the world of enlightenment, you have to expend a certain amount of energy—gain it, conserve it, expend it—to place yourself into a high state of awareness or to get beyond all gravity, to get into the world of enlightenment, of samadhi. Once you're there, you just let go. You're absorbed in perfect, radiant light. And as you go into the light, into the planes of light which lie beyond the physical dimensions and the astral dimensions, as you enter what we call the *causal dimensions* or the planes of light, you will be purified, energized, and you will become wise.

Wisdom in the world of enlightenment is not something that you gain through conversation. A certain amount of instruction can be gained in conversation, but wisdom and enlightenment is something that you gain by making the mind still. You can make your mind still, when you're alone, through the practice of meditation. If you learn some meditation techniques, you can quiet the mind; you can bring the kundalini up through the seven chakras and enter into various states of enlightened mind. If you meditate with a teacher who is enlightened, you can go higher, deeper. You can ride with them into stages of mind, into the nexus of the universe, that are perhaps not available to you at this time.

All of us have an aura, a body of energy, and that aura is linked to different planes of awareness. Some of us have the ability to access more planes of awareness than others because of our accomplishments in past lives, because of our practice in this life.

An enlightened teacher is someone who has an access not only to the astral dimensions but to the planes of light and beyond the planes of light to enlightenment itself, to nirvana. Nirvana is the highest, cleanest, purest and best of all things. And if you meditate with an enlightened teacher, if you sit with them and silence your mind as they go into nirvana, as they experience the clear light, the suchness, the thatness of perfect radiant oneness with all being, you will be, according to your lucidity, according to how well you meditate, able to travel with them. The pure power of their aura will bring you on a metaphysical journey into the world of perfection.

A teacher is really invaluable, as is personal practice. Each day you should meditate twice a day, in the morning and evening, and still your mind. A teacher will instruct you in chakra meditation, in how to silence the mind and raise the kundalini. A teacher will also instruct you in how to stabilize your energy field, increase it, decrease the loss of energy in your life—how to be balanced, how to have power and how to be wise and how to be funny, of course. It's a testing process, really—a testing process with yourself and a testing process with your teacher.

The purpose of enlightenment is certainly not the teacher, nor is it you. It doesn't have a purpose. Enlightenment simply exists, and if you would like to reach it, if you would like to attain it, if you would like to go beyond suffering, pain, frustration and the limited happiness that can be experienced in any form, then you need to journey to enlightenment. Individual practice is to meditate twice a day, and when you are not meditating to groom your mind, to eliminate hate, doubt, fear, anxiety, negative thoughts, emotions and stages of awareness that limit your consciousness, that bind you to a sense of self, of ego.

This is the practice of mindfulness, of monitoring your mind all day and all night. It's enjoyable to just simply remove things that make you unhappy from your mind, to clarify your emotions and to lead a happy and productive life. Then you need to see your teacher, to sit in meditation with them, to take journeys with them to high energy places—places of power where it's easier to meditate, where it's easier to access higher dimensions. The relationship with a teacher is not really a relationship. A teacher of enlightenment is enlightened and they simply express enlightenment in their life by living. It's the student's responsibility and job to gain the teachings. It isn't the teacher's. The teacher's job is just to be perfectly enlightened.

In this era, we've grown to have a sense that it is the responsibility of the teacher to cause the student to learn. We've placed the burden on the teacher. And certainly it is the responsibility of the teacher to have knowledge and to teach it, and communicate it intelligently and effectively. But it is not the responsibility of the enlightened teacher to bring the student to enlightenment. That may be true in the classroom—in algebra, in trigonometry, in computer science, in English, in art. I don't know. Each teacher has their own philosophy in each school.

But in the world of enlightenment, it is not the responsibility of the teacher. It's your responsibility. You're the one that wants enlightenment, and you have to do what's necessary to find it—enter into it. And to do that, you have to let go of everything. You have to let go of your ideas about enlightenment, your ideas about teachers and teachings, your ideas about yourself. You have to be responsible, conscious, and above all, earnest—not perfect, far from perfect. But you need to have a sincere, earnest interest in becoming one with the light, becoming fully conscious. And if you have that and you're flexible, you're accommodating, you're willing to follow your teacher's suggestions, then if your teacher is truly enlightened, if they have the power and the wisdom and the balance and the sense of humor necessary, you'll make rapid progress into the world of enlightenment.

Enlightenment is something that is real. And as I said, enlightenment is a journey. It's a journey through the ten thousand states of mind—a journey that is not accomplished in a single day or moment. Each time you meditate, you take the journey. Each time, you become more conscious, you love more, you feel more, you increase your depth. Each time, you gain a happier sense of what it is to live. Each time, you gain a little more control over your life. Each time, when you don't, you don't allow that to discourage you and cause you to give up—you become a little more enlightened.

Enlightenment is cumulative, in other words. You become a little more enlightened each day as you practice yoga and Buddhism. But simply having a teacher and doing what you call meditation will not necessarily bring you to enlightenment. You can sit and just space out and not meditate. A lot of people do that and they think they're doing a wonderful meditation. You can become pompous and egotistical and think that you're very important and think that is a spiritual achievement.

There is no such thing as spiritual achievement. While enlightenment—while people who are enlightened, fully enlightened—in this world are rare, it's not an achievement. It's not a belt ranking. It's simply an awareness that's intrinsic to all life that they have managed to gain or become conscious of. It's certainly worthy of our respect because life is worthy of our respect. But to put them on a pedestal is a mistake. To undervalue them is also a mistake.

In other words, you have to come to the world of enlightenment with open hands, that is to say, not clenched in fists, without an agenda. You'll have an agenda, of course, and you'll have your fists clenched—that is to say, you'll have expectations, ways you think it should work out, what you're going to receive from the experience. You'll have ideas about what you'll do and what you won't do. You can't help but have those things. But what matters the most is that you have a sincere love of truth.

There is something in you that loves light and you are willing to side with that part of your being more than any other side, and you are willing to be patient and go through the training, to go through the enlightenment cycle. You're not vain enough to think that you will necessarily become fully enlightened in this lifetime. It doesn't really matter. There's no time factor. Yet you would like to become as fully conscious as possible in this life, before death, because it makes life more enjoyable to be fully conscious, and also, in your next lifetime, you get that consciousness back. It returns to you, partially at the moment of birth and, as you are drawn back to meditation, fully.

It's something that you can't lose. In this lifetime, you can lose everything. You can amass a fortune and it can be lost. You can have a healthy body and it can get sick. People you love can leave you or experience misfortune, and they can die. Everything passes here. And when you leave this world, you lose the body that you've developed down at Gold's Gym. You lose the mind that you've educated at the universities. You lose everyone and everything. But you don't lose enlightenment or any spiritual knowledge that you've gained in this or any other lifetime. It's inside you. It's in potential. The answer is to bring it back, to become more conscious, more aware.

Enlightenment, as I said, is a journey. It's a journey that's made alone. It's a journey that's made with a teacher. It's also a journey that's made with friends, with other people who are practitioners, who are practitioners of yoga and Buddhism. As you meditate, it's good to have people around you who are doing the same thing because you help each other not take it too seriously, and yet you can cause each other to be inspired by each other's journeys.

Enlightenment is not about being political. It's not a social club. Ashrams often turn into that, I know. And societies of enlightenment often just become cliques. They often just become places where there's a hierarchy and a pecking order and not much enlightenment, but so what? That's what those people are drawn to. They need, I guess, to go through those experiences. But that has nothing to do with enlightenment. Enlightenment is the experience of light. It's something that you experience twice a day, when you meditate in the morning and evening. It's something that you experience in between those times because in your meditation you open your awareness field to a higher degree of light, and then you experience that light and increase it through the practice of mindfulness throughout the day.

To be completely aware, to be beautifully conscious, is the journey to enlightenment, and there's pain in it and there's suffering and there's frustration. But you already have those things, so it doesn't really matter. But there's ecstasy beyond comprehension. My suggestion, if you're drawn to the world of enlightenment, if you're interested in it, most of all, is to learn to meditate, not just to read a lot of books about it, not just to talk to people about it—those things are inspiring, perhaps. But the key to all enlightenment is to have personal experiences in the world of light. And all you need to do that is to meditate twice a day; to learn to practice mindfulness; to lead a simple, economical life; to work happily at whatever your tasks are and to use them to help you achieve perfection. And if you're able to have a teacher, to be with that teacher, to follow their instructions to the letter, if not more so—about how to meditate, how to lead a balanced life, how to gain power, wisdom, to have a sense of humor—the things they show you.

And you must be accommodating with your teacher. It is not the job of the teacher—it is not their responsibility—to cause you to be enlightened. It is your responsibility to do that. And so your responsibility means that you have to have a sense of humor about your teacher and the impossible things they ask you to do. They seem impossible to you only because you haven't done them. But the teacher will show you, if you're a good student, if you're patient—or maybe even if you're a bad student and you're impatient—how to increase your capacity to do things, how to do things that seem impossible. At five, it might have seemed impossible that someday you'd read and write and work and go to the university and do all the things you might do today. But you do them now, and it's no big deal.

An enlightened teacher is someone who has powers, who has awareness fields and access to them, who can do things that would seem impossible to the average person. They can—I guess what you'd say—perform miracles, although the real miracle is that the gold light of enlightenment, the pure light, shines through them. And that isn't their miracle. That's the miracle of enlightenment that's available to all of us.

With a teacher it's necessary to be sensitive to their directions. Most of the time they won't say much. They just walk around and they're enlightened. And you have to be very still and silent to understand what they're saying, that is to say, to see how they open the dimensions and to learn how to do that yourself. All the physical teachings, all the exoteric teachings, the things that can be discussed and explained, are only designed to give you the type of life that will allow you to practice the esoteric teachings. The exoteric or outer teachings show us different techniques and methods for achieving the kind of life that will allow us to enter into higher planes of awareness and become enlightened.

The esoteric or inner teachings, which only an enlightened teacher can deal with, are experiences in infinite awareness, experiences in infinite consciousness. They are the journey to enlightenment, the esoteric experiences, or the experience you will have with your teacher when they meditate and when, through the personal power of the kundalini, they empower you and lift you into higher dimensional plateaus, into fields of light. In other words, the esoteric teachings aren't something that you can express. They are the experiences in the planes of light, in the causal realities. And you go to a teacher not just to learn the teachings of how to live a happy, balanced life and optimize the possibilities of having spiritual experiences, but if the teacher is really enlightened, simply being around them is a spiritual experience. And then your job is to go home and learn to meditate and achieve those states on your own. Go back and see them, and they'll take you further, deeper, make more suggestions. And then you have to go back and be able to do those things on your own again.

A teacher is not someone who you have to have. That is to say, you don't need them perpetually. You need them to show you how to get through the doorway, but once you get through the doorway, you're on your own. Then you have to grow and experience enlightenment. And then you come back—if you want to go through a higher doorway—and so on and so on. Then they show you how to refine yourself until you're able to enter into nirvana on your own. And then no more teacher. Guess what? Only enlightenment everywhere. At the beginning and the middle and the end of all things, there's only perfection. And that's the perfection of enlightenment that is nirvana. That is here. Right now.

CHAPTER SEVEN

PERSONAL HAPPINESS

Happiness is the most elusive thing, it seems, for human beings to find. Happiness is something that everybody wants, or professes to want, so it must be a very difficult thing since so few people—relatively few people—seem to ever experience it. And if they do experience it, they sure don't seem to experience it for very long.

I'm the happiest person I have ever met—plain and simple.

The reason I'm happy is because I have a very good relationship with life. My happiness is not dependent upon what happens to me today or tomorrow or what happened yesterday. My happiness is dependent upon light. And since light is endless, since light is infinite, since light—the inner light, of course, of self-discovery, of enlightenment—is happiness in itself, then if I can make myself available to light, which I certainly do, then I'm bound to be happy. Always.

Life is a game that we play. It's a game in which happiness is the goal. Now, most people think happiness comes from experiences in the world. Possessions, they believe, bring them happiness—money, fame, fortune, personal relationships, achievements and accomplishments.

And certainly, all of these things can bring a measure of happiness to a person's life. For a while, the fulfillment of desire causes a type of happiness. But as soon as the experience passes, the happiness passes. Human beings are on a desire-aversion operating system—and if you understand the fallibility of this system, then you understand also that there is another system which is far superior—it's really not that hard to be happy.

The desire-aversion operating system works in the following way. When you want something, when you have a desire for something—a desire for food, a desire for sex, a desire for achievement, a desire for a new car, a new life—or when you have an aversion—you want to get away from something, you're afraid of something that makes you uncomfortable, you just simply don't like it—you are immediately in a problematic situation. Because your happiness, your state of mind, in other words, the way you feel, is based upon something extremely physical, and your happiness is now a victim to fortune, and fortune is capricious, that's for sure. If you want a new car, and if you get it, you'll be happy until the car isn't so new. And if you can't get it, you'll be unhappy. Or if you get it and somebody smashes into it, you're unhappy. Or if it isn't what you thought it might be, you're unhappy.

And sometimes there are things that make you unhappy, what you call aversions—things that you don't want in your life, that you don't like about yourself, that you just simply, at this time, can't get away from, try though you will. And if your happiness is dependent upon always getting everything that you desire and always avoiding everything that you want to avoid, chances are you won't be happy, or certainly not very often. This is the human system—desire and aversion.

Even the fulfillment of desire doesn't necessarily make you happy because there's a satiation factor. You can really love apple pie and get some apple pie and eat it, and you feel good for a minute. Then you can say, "Well heck, I felt good eating that apple pie. Why not eat ten? If this is what makes me happy, let me just keep doing it." But after a while, if we do the same thing in the same way over and over, repetitively, we get a sense of satiation. It just doesn't feel good any more. It doesn't taste as good. We're not happy. Even desire, if taken to an extreme, doesn't necessarily make us happy. It tends to make us actually rather cynical.

What makes us happy and what increases happiness is contact with light. The experience of light in a very pure form, if not the purest form, always creates happiness. And the experience of desire and aversion tends to create unhappiness. In the world of light, that is to say, as you have experiences with the inner light, which are gained through the practice of meditation and Buddhism, as you experience light, it immediately delights you.

Within the universe there is pure light. It's a light that is beyond all darkness, and it does not give way to anything. It is the light of existence. It's the clear light of reality, the *dharmakaya.* The very nature of the light is happiness. When you experience the light, voila! You're happy. You don't have to do anything, be anybody special, have a series of accomplishments behind you. If you can get there, you're happy—if you can experience the light. The more often you experience the light, the deeper your immersion in the light, the happier you become.

In other words, it's an object orientation mindset to a certain extent. That is to say, there is the light. There is the experience of the light. The light by its very nature is endless. It has no beginning. It has no end. Therefore you can never say that you've had the ultimate experience in light—so there is no ultimate level of happiness, it goes on forever.

The light is not quantifiable. It just is. And you experience it in meditation when thought stops, when you go beyond the senses. When you go beyond the limitations of the ego, the light is waiting for you.

Your experiences in the light become stronger, they become happier, and you experience it more frequently as you progress along the pathway to enlightenment. The pathway to enlightenment is happiness. And it really doesn't matter what's going on in your physical life—if you're successful, if you're in prison, if you're dying, if you're being born, if you're somewhere in the middle—it really doesn't matter, if you have contact with light.

Physical circumstance will not cause happiness. Or if it does, it immediately places you in jeopardy because once you've gained happiness from something that occurred to you, something you've gotten, something that you've attained, there's the fear of loss. The loss of that thing, the object of desire which makes you happy—now you're a slave to it. You've become bound to it.

Let's say that your wife or husband, boyfriend, girlfriend, makes you happy, or your dog or your cat. If your happiness just comes from being in contact with them, if they leave you, you're bound to be unhappy. You'll be depressed. You'll be miserable. Now you're their slave. You're the slave of the thing that makes you happy. You have to do whatever it takes to keep it around you all the time. You're a junkie, and human relationships can be expensive habits. Career achievement can be an expensive habit. Anything can be an expensive habit. And you're always afraid of losing it. Once you've attained something, there is the fear of loss, if that's what causes your happiness.

The enlightened alternative is to be happy because you experience light. And then you can be married or not, have children or not, be successful or not. You can play in the world, and if you gain happiness from something, great! If you don't, it won't bother you because your happiness is so large, it's so great, it's so immeasurable, that you simply won't be bothered by what goes on in the physical world.

I recommend to my students to make a lot of money. It seems that human beings have problems with money. Most of human life seems to revolve around the getting of money or that which money brings. And when people have problems with money, they cut back. They say to themselves, "Well, we don't have as much as we used to, so we'll have to cut back on the things that we enjoy." I don't think that's the answer. I don't think economizing is the answer. For example, the United States has an incredible national debt. Now, it's good to economize in the sense that waste is waste. That's obviously not the way to live, and you have to eliminate waste in your life as the United States has to eliminate waste in its spending, so it isn't a deficit government.

But the answer for the United States, or the answer for an individual, is to make more money. If the country is bringing in more money than it's sending out, or even if it's at an even point, then there's balance. If you're having problems with money, the answer isn't cutting back. I mean, you have to have the things you have to have—anything else is an extra, it's an add-on, and maybe you need it and maybe you don't. Sometimes we get out of proportion, and we think that we really need more than we need because we think it will make us happy. And that's not true. But you do need whatever it is you need—to work, to live, to function—at whatever level is appropriate for you.

But the answer is to make more money. I suggest to my students that they go into computer science—unless they have a better field—because it's the most lucrative of all fields, and to make absolutely a ton of money. And then money simply isn't a problem. They don't have to spend their life always worrying about whether they have enough to cover expenses. Many people do that, and they experience so much unhappiness. The obvious answer to money is to have tons of it. And so, if you know that that's the answer to dealing with the physical world, then simply you figure out how to make more money than you really need and go do it. It's really not that impossible.

In other words, sometimes we just have to get a clear sight of something, and if it's so important, why don't we just figure out what we need to do and go do it? We have to step back from the problem and evaluate it. It seems to me that in life all you really need are a healthy body, a healthy mind, a healthy spirit and a bunch of money. That is to say, money equals the ability to be mobile in this world—to travel, to live in a place that's suitable, to not to be brought down or drained, not to be a victim.

I equate the inner light with that also. I mean, it's the same operating system. Rather than economizing or figuring how to get by on a budget, why not just have tons of money? Why not have tons of happiness? Why not become so happy that no matter what happens in life as you journey, doing the things that are appropriate for you, that if it all falls apart it doesn't matter because you're happy. That's, I think, the happiness equation—is just to be so happy, to figure out how one becomes happy and to go do it—that fortune is not a problem. You can always just fall back on your inner happiness.

And if you had a day where it went your way, great. But you hardly notice because you're so happy because you meditate. And if you have a day where it all falls apart, then it really is insignificant because you're so happy. And when death comes along, it isn't a fearful thing because you're so happy and knowledgeable from the pursuit of meditation that you're simply not afraid. You can see what lies beyond it. You know that life is good—what makes us is good, and we are what makes us—and there is nothing to fear. And even sickness becomes an experience that we pass through in happiness because our happiness is not dependent upon how our body feels, but how our spirit feels.

Yoga, that is to say, Buddhism, is the study of how to be immeasurably happy. And a long time ago, individuals, through inner study and by examining life, realized that the way to happiness is through meditation, introspection—that happiness already exists somewhere in the universe. They looked at life and they saw that most people aren't happy, or their experiences with happiness come and go, as do their desires and aversions and the fate that meets them. And they saw that this was obviously an inefficient system. They combed the universe and found that there is immeasurable happiness inside of us, not inside of our physical persons, but inside of our spirits.

We're immortal spirits. We live forever. And within the spirit, within that which is eternal in us, there's a place where there's infinite happiness. And you can get to it, just like you can go to the refrigerator for food. And it's always abundant and it's always there. Now, I am not being optimistic or euphemistic or unreal in any sense.

Most people are just completely oblivious to eternity. They look at the sky and the stars at night, and they think that's eternity. That's just the senses having contact with the sense world. Outside of the physical dimension, there are other dimensions. There are astral dimensions and there are the causal dimensions. The causal dimensions are the dimensions of light, the planes of light. Happiness is in the physical dimensions, in a limited way, in the astral dimensions in a limited way, but it's in the causal dimensions in an unlimited way. The causal dimensions, which I refer to as the planes of light, are happiness. They're all different and they're endless. And they, of course, border the shores of nirvana, which is beyond discussion, which goes beyond happiness itself to something else—a condition of such perfection that it cannot be expressed.

Meditation is the journey to happiness. As you meditate and as you enter into the planes of light, you'll become happy, immediately happy. That happiness will enable you to compact your life, transform yourself and open yourself to those planes—not just when you're meditating but eventually all of the time, so that you're in a perpetual state of meditation. That is to say, you can be in this world physically and have all the myriad experiences that life has to offer, and at the same time yoke your awareness field, join your consciousness to the planes of light and eventually to nirvana itself. You can create a conscious opening and go back and forth between these places.

While you are at work, typing at the keyboard or doing whatever it is you do, or at school or playing or doing some sports, athletics, when you are in a very difficult situation where everybody is pounding on you because they're not too happy, or you are just doing something bright and beautiful—at those times while you are physically engaged in your activities, your mind can be wandering through the planes of light forever, having constantly new and greater experiences that cause you happiness.

The trick to being happy is to get beyond the body, not just to the astral realms. The astral realms don't necessarily make you happy. There are people who have access to the astral realms. But in the astral realms they are still who they are here, and that doesn't create happiness. Going to the astral worlds is just like going to another country. You are who you are here, and when you go to another country, you're the same person there.

But when you go into the causal realms, into the realms of light, at that time you become someone else. The nature of the causal realms is pure light. The light vibrates very quickly. And to be in the causal realms, to be in the planes of light, to experience them, it washes away the parts of yourself that cause unhappiness and pain. Or perhaps it might be more correct to say that it provides us with a better understanding of who we are.

And you will come to see that you are not necessarily the body or the person who has the experiences. Nor are you the personality, the ego, that reacts with pride or with anger or with hope. You're not necessarily the body of desires, the thoughts, the memories. You see that you're a field of light, an endless field of light, a concurrence of light, and that light, for a while, has taken shape and form in the body that you now occupy, in the universe that appears to your senses, and it experiences the play of life—the emotions, the dramas, the soap opera of existence.

Real happiness comes from the experience of meditation and from getting to a point where you like life. You can enjoy it, but you don't center your happiness on what happens here. Meditation is a direct and vivid encounter with immortality. It's not a ritual. It's not based upon wishful thinking. It's something that you go and do. It's like swimming. And you jump in the water and there you are. You're swimming. It's an actual, very visceral experience. But the experience of meditation, the experience of the planes of light, which I would define as the experience of meditation, changes you. That is to say, it causes all the blockages, the meanness, the unhappiness, the self-destructive tendencies, to pass. When you take a shower, all the dirt is washed off. When you go into the planes of light, all the incorrect ideas, the incorrect ways of seeing and understanding life that you pick up along the way, on the journey, are washed away.

If you go into the planes of light in the morning and in the evening in your meditation, then you wash everything away that you've picked up. But you also gain ground, in a sense, because as you go into the planes of light, more light comes back with you each time you meditate. You get better at meditation. And each morning when you meditate, you can experience a deeper ecstasy. Each evening when you meditate you can experience a more profound reality. You can have a better understanding of life. In other words, the planes of light certainly give you power, the power to rise above circumstance, the power to rise above your desires and your aversions to happiness.

Your experiences in the planes of light will create a balance, a happiness in your life—just in simple things. But it gives you the wisdom, it gets you out of the trap of self. The trap of self is the trap that causes unhappiness. It's the thing we get stuck in. We define ourselves too much. We're very sure of who we are and what we're doing. And we're so sure, that we're not very happy. Whereas the infinite intelligence of the universe, which is what we truly are—the pure light, the pure radiant spirit—is not so definable. It can take every form or no form. It can be all of this and something else that we don't know.

When you meditate and you still your mind, when you relax a little bit and chill out and let go of the desires and the aversions for a while and enter into the light—if you do it with your full being, with your full body and mind and spirit, you'll be purified. You'll be energized, but you will also become wise. You will gain the wisdom, the knowing of things in this world, in other worlds and beyond worlds. It just comes to you.

The way we gain wisdom in meditation is not by having someone explain something to us. All the teacher does is explain how to get to the planes of light, how to go deeper into them, how to avoid the things that keep you out of them. And of course, an enlightened teacher, a fully empowered teacher, can lift you into the planes directly so that you can become more familiar with them and get to them sooner and more frequently. They speed up the educational process. But that's all an enlightened teacher does. They teach you to laugh, to be balanced. But they don't give you wisdom. You might gain some wisdom by observing how they act and react—wisdom of a certain kind. But real wisdom is gained personally in meditation. It's something that you will gain in the planes of light.

No one quite knows how it works, meaning it can't be expressed in words. But when you meditate, if you can stop thought or even distance yourself from thought and go into the planes of light, or have the planes of light enter you, you will come out of the meditation knowing things—things that perhaps are inexpressible. You might learn how to move through the dimensions. You might learn how to dissolve the self. You might learn how to use the siddha powers to heal, to do all kinds of things. That's one kind of knowledge. You might learn just to be bright and clear and aware, to be more conscious, to be funny. Or you might gain the wisdom of immortality, the knowledge that life has, which is inexpressible.

Meditation is the short path to happiness. It is the way to become completely happy. It streamlines the process. It takes you beyond the desire-aversion operating system which offers very limited happiness and a great deal of frustration. Meditation, as you practice meditation—it's no good just to talk about it but you need to do it—if you can bring an earnestness to your meditation, if you can really try, in other words, you will find that happiness is something that will run through your life constantly.

At first, when you begin the practice of meditation, of course, your happiness will be limited because you can't get that deeply into the planes of light. But through the practice, you'll gain a little bit of happiness, and that will inspire you to meditate more. And with consistent practice, you will gain access to the planes of light, particularly if you have a teacher who is enlightened, who will guide you and make sure that you're getting into the planes of light and not into the astral. Then each day, as you progress along the pathway, you will be happier. And then you can go live your life, have your career, enjoy your sports, do whatever is necessary, but you will find that happiness will not be elusive. It'll be who you are.

If you sit down and meditate in the morning, you will be filled with happiness, and that happiness will last you all day. Then, in the evening, you'll meditate again, and you'll wash away any of the debris you picked up during the day—wrong views, that sort of thing—that can lead to unhappiness. And you'll be filled and flooded with a different kind of happiness, the happiness of the evening. And then you'll be happy all night. Meditate in the morning and wash away anything you picked up in the dream state. It's a cycle, the enlightenment cycle. It's based on meditation.

The role of the teacher is to make sure that the practice is pure, that is to say, that the methods are taught properly. And by giving proper empowerments and by guiding the student, you make sure that they really are going into the planes of light and they're not fooling themselves. Because the astral, and the astral dimensions are not places of great happiness necessarily. As I said, they're just like journeying to another country. The teacher has to make sure that the student is truly meditating and that the student is progressing in their meditation, and provide the empowerments and the instruction necessary to do that. That's all. That's what true teaching is, to make sure the student is on the path and that the path is leading to deeper and greater light.

Then the rest is up to the light. As you go into the light, it will cause you to become happier and happier. And each day, you will gain a deeper happiness, a more subtle or perhaps a more profound happiness, and that happiness will free you from the desire-aversion cycle or syndrome.

It sounds pretty good, doesn't it? It is. It's better than it sounds. And it's such a simple thing that people miss it. It's worth your while to sit, to practice meditation—if happiness is one of the important things in your life. It's like making money. Make too much of it, and money is certainly not a problem—less of a problem. If you are just too happy, if you have an abundance of happiness, then life is bright. We see it more correctly.

Unhappiness is really an incorrect seeing. When we're unhappy, we don't see life as it really is. It means that we are not in a condition of light. We're in a condition of veiled light, of shadows. We don't see very well, and what we think is, isn't. In the dark, you can't see. You bump into things and you mistake them for something else. You stumble across a rope and think it is a snake, and you get scared to death. Or maybe it's a snake, and you think it's a rope and think you're safe.

In light, we can see what is and what is not. We know what's right and what's inappropriate—right in the sense that it is truly the essence of all things, the suchness, the *dharma,* the ultimate good. And if we immerse ourselves in the ultimate good, it will free us from all limitations, from all sorrows, from all ignorance, and we'll have this silly smile on our face or perhaps just inside our hearts. And that's what illumination is.

Illumination, at least in the outer world, is to be happy, no matter what's going on—whether you're successful or whether you're a failure, whether you're up or you're down, you're in or you're out. That's truly illumination in the outer world. In the inner world, it's different. It's more profound. It's more ineffable. It's harder to express.

So be happy. Always be positive because that means you are seeing things correctly. And if you are negative, if you're depressed, if you are unhappy, that simply means that you are not seeing life in its perfection. Rather than being frustrated about it, sit down and meditate. Clear your mind, be patient, follow the instructions of an enlightened teacher in your meditation practice, and then you will come to know all things and be free from all limitations and be happy. It's really that simple.

CHAPTER EIGHT

REINCARNATION

Reincarnation is a dance. It's a movement of life to the rhythm of the universe. The idea is simple. There is spirit and there is matter, and they join together—one as one dancing partner and one as the other. The two together make a dance. They're together for a time while they're on the dance floor, and then they separate and go their individual ways for a while. And then they come together and dance again, and it goes on forever.

The spirit, the eternal part of our being, is indescribable and limitless. We are eternal spirits. As spirits we have always existed in a generalized form, since we are all part of the universe, the spirit of the universe. As individual spirits, we've existed for a timeless time. And in that time, we have participated in the dance of reincarnation. Reincarnation means simply that we have lived before, we live now and we'll live again, that there is no end to life and that death is only a brief pause in our journey. It's a rest. When we have reached the end of a lifetime, we rest. The dancers take a break. And then off we go again, with a new partner, with a new body, with a new life.

Reincarnation is a cyclic process. The idea is that there are endless levels of creation, different universes, you might say, or dimensions. And in each one, something similar is taking place, evolution, the evolution of spirit through matter. Now, to say that matter and spirit are different is a way of talking. It's a way of trying to discuss something. They're not necessarily different in that they both come from the eternal light. And the *samsara,* the world of experience, temporal experience, and *nirvana,* the world of enlightenment, are really one. That's an apprehension that you will have some day in the world of enlightened experience. But for discussion purposes, it's certainly a lot easier to separate them.

Reincarnation is a process that's going on in endless dimensions. But let's just look at our own because, while the forms differ, the process is the same. If we can understand how one city works, while it won't tell us how all cities are or all about them, it'll give us a central understanding that's probably applicable in most situations.

In this universe, meaning the world of the earth that we live on, people are at different levels of evolution. They may all have human bodies, but the souls are different. Some souls are more advanced. Some souls are less advanced—advanced in the sense that they are more aware of their possibilities. Advanced souls seek enlightenment. Souls that are not as advanced seek happiness and pleasure in sensorial experience. The more advanced soul has learned that happiness, that fulfillment, doesn't really come from simply leading a physical life. It can be enjoyable. It can be painful. It can be a combination of both.

But real happiness comes from absorption in the world of spirit, in the world of light, in the worlds of enlightenment.

The advanced soul is really the discussion point in our journey through reincarnation. Your interest in the subject would suggest that you are more advanced than most individuals because most individuals on earth are not drawn to the higher light at this time. That doesn't in any way make you, or anyone who's interested in such things, superior to anyone else. If you're in eighth grade, you're not better than someone who's in the fourth grade. You were in fourth grade, now you are in eighth. The people in fourth will one day be in eighth. It's a progression.

But what's interesting about reincarnation, from the point of view of the more advanced soul, let's say, is how the process works, that is, "Where am I? What are my possibilities? Is there some way that I can know this system better so that I can gain more out of it?" That's the perspective of the more advanced soul. And our concerns are really twofold. One is the experience of this life, and the other is the experience between lifetimes. The experience of the next life is too far away to really be concerned with, and it will be an outgrowth of this incarnation and what happens between birth and death.

There's not much we can do about past lives. They're done. There is not much we can do about our future life in that it hasn't occurred yet. But our knowledge and our experience, our wisdom, can assist us in gaining more from this life, which will correctly set up our next life.

And of course, it can also assist us during the intermediate stage of the bardo plane, when we're between lives, between birth, death and rebirth, in between all things.

If in this life you have a sense that you have lived before—it's a feeling, it's an understanding, a knowing, a silent knowing—this is a very helpful thing because it enables you to deal happily with our day-to-day lives, with your day-to-day life. If you know that you've lived before, that you've had many, many lives, countless lives, then what happens in this life is not quite as traumatic. If this is the only life that you lead, then everything assumes a great importance, perhaps too great an importance. We have to get everything out of life and perhaps we overdo it. If today you're alive and you suspect you'll be alive tomorrow, we enjoy today but there will be a tomorrow, and we don't have to fit everything into today. We don't have to have every experience today. We don't have to know every happiness or have every piece of knowledge today because there is tomorrow.

When you know that there are future lives, it's not necessary for you to cram everything into this lifetime. You can enjoy this lifetime, follow your interests, go with the flow of your life and know that it will lead you to a better life in your next incarnation. Reincarnation is the journey of hope because in each lifetime, we move forward to a place that's better than our last lifetime, a place inside of ourselves, an awareness. Think of reincarnation as school. When you go to school you're in first grade, and then there's the summer vacation. Then there's second grade and the summer vacation. You don't go back to the previous grade, of course, unless you failed the course. And if you do, you take those courses again and then move on. In summer vacation is a respite. It's a chance just to relax, to have fun, to do something different because you just can't keep learning all the time. You don't learn much. After a while you burn out.

Reincarnation works something like that. In this lifetime, you are at the level of your current awareness. That's your subject. The subject you are studying today is your life, and what can you do with the fabric of the life that you have, to become happier, to become more knowledgeable, to become more balanced, to become more free. How can you use that fiber, that texture? How can you change it? How can you interact with it, to get to a better place, a place you enjoy more, inside your mind?

If you do well with this life, then that knowledge, that awareness, will be held within you, within the causal structure, the part of us that lives from one lifetime to another. And it will be available to you in your next life and in future lives, not necessarily at the moment of birth. But if you meditate, it will come back to you. If, in this lifetime, you don't meet the challenge, you don't learn anything new, if you just kind of veg-out in this lifetime, in this incarnation, then you'll be right back in the same place in your next life. Then you can take another shot at it.

Knowing about reincarnation helps us relax, in other words. It helps us enjoy what we enjoy, and it assists us with an understanding of death and dying. When we see someone that we love dying, it's not an ending. It's just another step, or maybe a new beginning. And while we're sad to see our friends go away for summer vacation, there's a sense that we can be with them again—if that is something we would like to do. And certainly, there is no sense of loss at death. Death is not an ending. Death is not the end, quite the contrary. Knowing this makes the journey through life—dealing with our own death and the deaths of those we love—much easier.

We can be alive and overcome this fear of death that seems to haunt so many people, particularly older people. Also, there is something we can do. We can gain more knowledge and more power in this lifetime. And even if sometimes in an incarnation you get a feeling of frustration—it's just not turning out the way you want it to on a physical level—if you pull your power together, if you meditate deeply, if you learn from life, if you study it, then no matter what happens to you physically—if your situation is good or bad—you will have gained from this life.

No lifetime is a loss if you've learned something, because that learning stays with you. And if you find yourself in very difficult or painful circumstances, if you can look on the bright side and if you can learn from these things, then there's no sense of loss. There's no such thing as a wasted life, if you've learned.

Reincarnation is the evolution of spirit through matter. Over thousands and millions of lifetimes, the soul evolves. It comes into light. The growth is slow. The progression is steady. All souls, however, do not reach enlightenment. Enlightenment exists within all souls and all things. But some souls reach a plateau, a certain peak, and then they stay there. Some souls actually decline at a certain point and go into different cycles. In other words, some people have the idea that reincarnation means, or the theory of reincarnation is, that the soul starts in a state of ignorance and eventually progresses to enlightenment, and that all beings eventually reach enlightenment—sentient beings, living beings. That's not true. That's a simplistic way of looking at it.

Life does not necessarily have a fixed purpose. It just is. It's an expression that's unknowable, beautifully unknowable. And for us to superimpose human points of view and try to shape it and format it so that we're comfortable with it, is interesting, but it's not necessarily accurate—nor does that imply that the knowledge of life is an uncomfortable thing to have. It's neither.

Some souls in their progression through incarnations reach a plateau, and that's a fine place to be. They stay there, you might say. They reach—after many, many lifetimes—a certain level of knowingness, and they just continue through lifetimes that are on that level. Life after life is about the same, but they like it that way.

Some beings do go down. That is to say, they forget. The soul falls into an eclipse of itself, and there is a downward progression for a time. Some souls attain enlightenment. They actually continue to go up into the highest gradients of light. No one knows why. You could say it's individual inclination. I'm not convinced that that's the case. It's just how the universe works.

But if we get above the individualized view of life, if we get above the individualized soul's journey, you will see that we're all one. We're all one light. We're all one essentiality. We're all one beautiful, perfect, essence. And in that sense, we are all enlightened. We are all one. We are all perfect perception. And yet in the outer manifestation of life, we take on different roles, we perform different tasks.

Souls have different journeys. The best thing to know is not what everybody else does but what you do. Self-discovery essentially is about finding your own *dharma,* your own rhythm—knowing that and pursuing it. And if you seek enlightenment, then what you need to know is there is a definite way to progress. There's a definite way to store and amass power, to re-awaken past life power, to continue your journey. And there's also a way to use the moment of death and the experience of the after-death plane to advance.

I'm not big, you might say, on the after-death experience. If you've done a very good job in your current lifetime, if you've put your time in, then your next lifetime will be set up for you. Think of it like school. At the university, if you study all semester and you do a good job, finals—if they're a cumulative exam—are not a big deal. You just have to lightly review because you've studied all along. When everybody else is stressing out and studying countless hours and getting mediocre grades, you'll get an A with a light review because you've been progressively on the case. That's the best way to be. It is possible to cram for a final exam, certainly. If you just have not gotten around to studying, you just might pull off a slightly better grade by doing a lot of work at the last minute. And that's essentially what the after-death experience is. That is to say, the yoga of the *bardo* plane, yoga of the after-death experience, is a way to try and slightly improve your grade because you haven't done everything that you should have done.

The best thing to do is—just do a good job in the first place. If you meditate, if you lead a clean life, if in spite of the egotism and vanity and jealousy and all the weird thoughts that pass through the mind and the personality; if in spite of these things you continue to have fun with yoga and with Buddhism; if you continue to be bright and positive and hopeful and to continually—no matter how many times you wander away from it—follow the pathway to enlightenment, then you will learn a great deal. You will amass more knowledge, and you will move to a higher incarnation. That is to say, in your next lifetime, you'll be much wiser than you were in this one, much happier, and you won't have to go through as much suffering. Or if you do go through suffering, you will be able to use it to advance yourself even further.

On the other hand, it's possible, as I said, if at the last moment you had not done perhaps all that you could have with your life, if you haven't really been on the case as much as you could be, it is possible at the last moment to make a tremendous transition—to go much higher, to experience eternity more directly and more completely by joining yourself in the *bardo* plane with the higher fields of enlightenment.

There is a book called *The Tibetan Book of the Dead.* And that book is really an instruction guide, it's a TripTik for the after-death experience. To a certain extent, it's very hard to understand in that it's written mainly in symbols, and if you have advanced quite far in the practice of yoga, you might be able to understand those symbols. But essentially, it's an instruction guide to recognize and pass—through a series of meditation practices at the time of death and after death—the *bardo* plane so that your next incarnation will be a higher incarnation. It's a difficult yoga to practice, to be honest with you, and it's something that only someone fairly adept in yogic practice to begin with can really pull off.

It's an interesting book to read, and I think actually a lot of knowledge of *The Tibetan Book of the Dead* is useful for the living because the experience of the *bardo* plane is not something that you're limited to at the time of death. Life is the *bardo.* I mean the experience of death is the experience of life, in a certain sense. The planes of consciousness that are available at the time of death are also available to the living, and the transmutations that can occur at the time of death can also occur while you're alive. It's useful in that sense both for the living and for the dead.

But as I have said before, the best thing to do is to do a good job with this life. If you have a sense of the timeliness of life, if you feel that, "Yes, I will be in another incarnation," and, "Yes, it does matter what I do in this incarnation," I think that's the best attitude. If you feel that you are under some tremendous pressure to do everything perfectly in this lifetime so you won't have a horrible incarnation in your next life—I think that's a little much, personally. I think that life is not that finicky, and I think that that type of fear is unnecessary.

Some people don't enjoy their life because they feel they're working hard and assiduously and reaping lots of good karma for their next lifetime. And I don't think that's an accurate understanding of the reincarnation process. It seems to me that happiness is something that you don't postpone. And if you're postponing happiness, it's something that you'll probably never experience much of.

Happiness is something that comes from creating good karma, and the monk or the individual who feels that, "Well, I'm working so hard for everybody else and for the salvation of everyone, and that's going to give me a great life in my next lifetime," and they have a sense that it's unpleasant to do what they're doing, is not really creating any good karma and will not really have a better lifetime than their current lifetime.

A better lifetime comes from not some karmic scale but from inner knowledge. And inner knowledge makes you happy. In other words, it's not as if someone is checking. There's the thought, among many yogis or practitioners, that there is some giant balance scale or record where someone is keeping track, like Santa Claus is supposed to do for Christmas, and it will determine the allotment of your presents according to how good or bad you were. And that's absurd. That's a very exoteric understanding of reincarnation. The esoteric understanding is that what you will be in your next life is the sum total of the realizations that you've had in this lifetime. And the realizations that you have in this lifetime are cumulative in that they increase as you grow older, if you keep practicing yoga. And if you are happier every day, that means you're practicing yoga. Your yoga, your Buddhism, is successful. And if you're not happier every day, if you don't feel better, if you don't see a progression of development from day to day, month to month and year to year in your life, then, well, you're certainly not practicing yoga or Buddhism—and therefore you can't be amassing any positive karma. Positive karma is a better mental state.

Self-honesty is absolutely necessary in the practice of Buddhism. And the main point of self-honesty that you need is to ask yourself, "Am I really practicing Buddhism? Am I really practicing yoga? Am I really happier? Do I feel better about my life? Do I feel more relaxed?" Even though the circumstances of life are sometimes pressured and chaotic, aside from that, just "Do I personally feel better? Have I reached a mental state this year that's vastly superior to the mental state I had last year?" If the answer is no, then you've got to start your yoga and your Buddhism over. You're not doing it right, and certainly your practice will not lend to a better incarnation or whatever you want to call it.

In other words, I think all incarnations are this incarnation. And the primary purpose of reincarnation, the knowledge of it, is that it assures us that life is worth living, that all this is not vain and futile, and that the spiritual practice that we do in any given life is not a waste of time. Life is not a one-shot deal. It is forever, and things do count. But to be so simplistic as to think that you can just go out and help a lot of people and somehow get a better life, that's not reincarnation as I know it. That's fantasy. A better life comes from being happy and from inner realizations. Now if helping others adds to that, well then, it's great. But postponing happiness—suffering, in other words, intentional suffering and the postponement of happiness—is not yoga or Buddhism, and it will not lead to a better incarnation.

If you'd like to have a better incarnation, then have one now. And if that's your attitude and you just let go and meditate and try to be as wise and compassionate, as understanding as you can—learn patience and the higher virtues, and if you enjoy them, if you have fun with it, that's yoga. That's Buddhism as I know it. And then the process simply gets more and more exciting, and the ecstasy gets deeper and that's what will go into your next life. That's who you will be born as—the person who's happy. While all the other babies are in the cribs in the delivery room, crying, you'll be smiling, I guess. Well, I don't know about that, but something like that. Have a sense of humor.

Reincarnation is not what a lot of people think. Yes, we are eternal. No, everyone does not attain enlightenment. It's not necessary. Life is smarter than we are. Whatever is supposed to happen, happens. We're dealing with the cosmos, and it has its own ways. To observe those ways and be in touch with them—that's wisdom. But to try and make it fit into a neat mental package—that's very unwise because you'll be very surprised when you discover that it doesn't work out that way, that that wasn't true. Your illusions will be painful for you.

The best use of reincarnation, the best knowledge of it, is the knowledge that gives us a better life today, now—a sense that death is not the end so we're not afraid of it, a sense that it does make sense to do a good job with our life because we have a happier life now and we'll be happier in the next life. To be afraid of our next life because, you know, we don't feel we've done a good job with this life, is not wise. It creates unhappiness now.

Your next life is another opportunity to learn what you didn't learn in this lifetime. In other words, the knowledge of reincarnation should relax you a little bit. At the same time, it should tell you that it is worth pursuing inner knowledge because that inner knowledge will make your next life more pleasant than this one was, certainly. But the knowledge of reincarnation is not a fearful thing. It's something that inspires you to be happy today, and it also, of course, shows you that through the practice of meditation and entering into the planes of light, you can pull all the past life realizations you've had into this life—or the ones that you need to make you strong and to give you the insight to go even further into higher bliss and into higher ecstasy, into greater laughter. That's the essence of reincarnation.

The essence of all reincarnation is to have the best lifetime now that you've ever had, no matter what's going on, on the earth or wherever you happen to be, and to not worry about your future life—to simply have a wonderful life now and to be as happy as possible. And happiness, of course, will come through the practice of yoga and Buddhism, by stilling the mind in meditation and by allowing the spirit to unfold. That happiness is not something you'll lose at the end of this lifetime. It will stay with you, and in your next lifetime you will be that much further ahead. It will be easier to get back to that place than it was this time, and you'll go further ahead.

Reincarnation is a hopeful understanding of life. It's an accurate understanding of life. In each lifetime we grow, develop and evolve. And as long as you continue to practice meditation and yoga, you will eventually reach the world of enlightened mind and be totally free and perfectly happy and knowledgeable.

Reincarnation is the happy news, the good news. Life is eternal, and it's worth living, and what we do in this life is not futile. Death is not the end. And our practice in this life will assist us in our next life, and if we don't come to a perfect understanding in this lifetime, it's not a problem. That's what the next life is for. And yes, you can cram for exams. You can read *The Tibetan Book of the Dead,* and if you skipped it in this lifetime, if you didn't do the job, you can try to pick it up at the end. But that's not our discussion point today.

CHAPTER NINE

CAREER SUCCESS

I'm a teacher of American Buddhism. American Buddhism is a new form of Buddhism. It's a little different from our practice in the Far East. In the Far East, Buddhism is usually practiced in a monastery. You enter a monastery, and you live your life there. And you get up at a certain time, you have meals at a certain time, and you tend the garden or copy manuscripts. You meditate at certain times. You study with the master or the teaching monks. It's a certain type of life. But in the West, while certainly there will be Buddhist monasteries, I'm sure, it seems to me the best form of practice is to live in the world, to have your own home or apartment, condominium, have your own car. It just seems to work better here.

The spirit of the West, of America, is different than the East. The cultural conditioning is very different, and it seems to be harder for people here to work in teams. It seems to be more difficult for people here to live in harmony, in a monastery. Certainly there are monasteries and convents have flourished in the Christian tradition for a long time in Europe and America and other places in the world. But a Buddhist monastery has a certain chemistry. There's a certain laughter, a certain excitement, a certain brightness and ebullience, and it's hard to capture that here. I think that same brightness here is captured in another way, and that's by living and working in the world. It's certainly more challenging in certain ways, and certainly about the same in other ways as compared to living in monasteries in the Far East.

As a practicing Buddhist in America and the West, or even in the Far East, in Japan and other places, if you don't live in a monastery then you have to have a job. Even in a monastery, of course, you have a job, usually. But here you have to live and work in the world, and most of the time that people spend in their lives is devoted to working, whether it's school or work. School is preparation for work and is a type of work, and then later we finish school and go to work. We get a job.

Working is not a nine-to-five experience. It's a lifetime. Most people get up around 6:00 to get ready for work, 6:30, some even earlier, some a little later. Off they go into traffic. They have to commute for an hour or two sometimes just to get to work, spend the day there, commute back. They have to make sure their clothes are ready for the next day. They might have to do some study for the next day if their job calls for it, particularly if they are in a supervising or managerial position, or an R & D position.

In other words, for most people, a tremendous amount of time goes into their work. It's the main thing that we do in life to sustain ourselves just as bodies. It's a very important thing and it consumes a great deal of our energy, and energy is the central study or the component theme of Buddhist practice, of yoga—is the conservation of energy. And that's why people live, or have lived, in monasteries. The idea was, the walls of a monastery are not to keep you in but to keep everybody else out because you want to develop a certain type of life and most people in the world have other ideas on the subject. Buddhists have, for a long time, lived in monasteries so that they can spend a certain amount of time working and a certain amount of time meditating. And they don't want to use up all their energy in working.

You might say living in a monastery cuts down the commutation time. That alone would give you a couple of extra hours a day to meditate and do all kinds of things. And in a monastery, you lead a relatively simple life. You don't need a lot of possessions. You don't have to work as many hours to sustain yourself so you have more time for play. And spiritual practice is not thought of as an arduous thing or a hard thing, but play. It's the fun of life.

You think of spiritual practice as hard work. Certainly there's an element of work involved in it. But if you think of it as unpleasant work, it's not spiritual practice as I know it. It has nothing to do with it. Spiritual practice is what you do at the end of the day, and you look forward to it, and you can't wait to get there. It's like the greatest date you've ever had. You get to go meditate. You get to go see your teacher. You get to go get involved with a project that's advancing your consciousness because the immediate result—not just the future result of spiritual practice, if it's genuine—is joy, immediate happiness, a deeper understanding of reality.

In the West, people spend most of their time and energy working, and it would be a difficult thing if we couldn't gain something more than just dollars and cents from working. Because if you meditate for an hour in the morning, you have to get up an hour earlier than everybody else. And if you need to meditate for an hour at night, well, gee, there's not much time but just to meditate and work. And the problem is, of course, you come home and you're so tired from work you don't have much energy to meditate and have a good meditation; unless you use work in a *tantric* way, unless you use work as a way of advancing yourself. And that's how I define career success.

Career success is using your daily work—schoolwork, work in the world, work at home, doing the laundry, doing anything, all physical tasks, cleaning the car, any kind of work, and specifically career itself—using career as a way, and scholastics, of advancing your mental state. Also, obviously, career success means making enough money to lead the kind of life you'd like to lead as a practicing Buddhist, to be able to live in the kind of house in the right energy area, to have the kind of car, or whatever it is that you need to shelter yourself from the abrasive forces of life that would be draining to you and would keep you in lower states of mind. The purpose of work is to make enough money to exclude the abrasiveness, to shelter yourself, to live well, in other words, and happily and successfully in a material sense. Also, with work you can make money to assist others—if you enjoy that—to pay for your own spiritual practice, to advance yourself and just to have fun. But, by and large, I define career success as using your work to advance yourself spiritually.

Now, you can do that with any kind of work. That is to say, if you use work as meditation, if work becomes meditation, then eight hours of work is eight hours of meditation. It's still important to do a morning and evening silent meditation, meaning a sitting meditation, because it's an entirely different level of experience. And by doing a proper meditation in the morning, a good sitting meditation, you will open yourself up to the planes of light and that will enable you to do a strong work meditation all day, just to be in high states all day. And then, of course, if you do that, when you come home, you'll be able to meditate well again because you won't be as exhausted as everyone else is because you've been gaining a kind of internal *chi* or power from your work. That's the secret.

Meditation comes in different forms, and the best form of meditation, of course, is the one that makes you smile the most, and that's the sitting meditation. But next is work. Work is a great way to meditate. There is a particular form of work that I recommend to people who practice meditation. It's computer science, being a computer programmer or systems analyst or working in the data processing field. The mental structures that are used in computer science, particularly in working with relational database and artificial intelligence, are very similar to exercises that are done in Buddhist monasteries. And when you're in school, if you're studying computer science, it's literally like studying Buddhism. That is to say, in Buddhism, in Buddhist practice in monasteries, there are many exercises that we do to develop our mental powers so that we can meditate extremely well and go into other dimensions and other states of mind that are ecstatic and lead to enlightenment. It's necessary, if you are really going to meditate well, to do those exercises, which is why people always lived in monasteries—so they'd have the time, as I said before—you know, cut down the commutation time. And also there's an environment that's helpful for practice, and teachers are available, and a certain amount of backup is available from other students and the environment.

But really, computer science is fascinating. Because in the study of it as a student, as you study computer science, you will find that it will develop your mind. It makes your mind very strong. And it's literally like doing Buddhist exercises all day long. And then, of course, as a profession it's wonderful because it gives you a tremendous amount of money. Computer science is a very lucrative field. It's a very clean field. It's a non-polluting field, programming. There is always a job anywhere in the world because there just don't seem to be a whole lot of people who want to do it. And you can make lots and lots of money so that you can meet all your expenses and do your Buddhist practice and just have a wonderful life in the material sense—aid others, if you'd like to do that. But, as you study computer science and as you work in the environment, you develop this wonderful mental acumen—particularly with relational database and, of course, systems analysis and artificial intelligence.

You see, Buddhism is the study of the way the mind works. And in the beginning, it's explained to the student as simply meditating, leading a happy, bright life, accessing higher energy fields, moving the kundalini through the chakras and so on. That's all true, of course, in the preliminary stages. But as you advance in practice, it's necessary to develop certain faculties of mental discrimination. One has to be able to hold a large number of relational concepts simultaneously in the mind, and in the more advanced states, it's necessary to be able to "grid", to literally unlock realities and dimensions with the power of your mind. It isn't just a physical power that does this. It's an intelligence. And you have to become very subtle to do this; your mind has to be extremely flexible.

In the Buddhist monasteries, in Buddhist practice, normally a great deal of time is spent practicing mandala meditation. You learn to visualize and hold simultaneous concepts, usually visual concepts, in the mind during meditation. And after many years of doing this, the mind is developed in a specific way that enables you to pass through the dimensions into the higher planes of light and into the enlightened stages of attention.

Relational database work, artificial intelligence and related fields in computer science, really involve the same mindset, particularly artificial intelligence. What we're doing in AI is creating a mind, hopefully as pure a mind as possible, for a computer. We are replicating the way the mind works. And the mathematical fields that are adjacent to computer science, chaos theory, things like that—and also just the ability to program at that level—requires a high degree of development. If you combine that with the practice of morning and evening meditation, you will advance very rapidly in spiritual practice, and at the same time, you will work in an environment that is not as draining as many careers are, and it's extremely lucrative and it's fun.

Essentially, computer science is, I think, the most misunderstood field there is. You are being paid $30 an hour, $50 an hour, $150 an hour, whatever it is, depending upon your level, to play games all day, to solve puzzles. And for a person who's interested in meditation, that's the way their mind works. That is to say, a person who has practiced meditation in past lives, who is interested in meditation, reincarnation and psychic development and related things in this lifetime, their mind works in a certain way because of their practices in past lives.

It's very easy for such a person to do or be successful at computer science. They have already developed the mindset in past lives. And while a certain amount of energy will have to initially be spent, certainly working at programming, working at learning the languages and just kind of getting that mindset back, once you get past a certain point you'll find that combined with, of course, your practice in meditation and streamlining your life and, you know, doing all the kind of correct, essential things that one does in Buddhism, you will find that your life and your computer science will progress, your spiritual life and your computer science will progress extremely, extremely, rapidly. They assist each other.

Think of it this way. Let us suppose that, in a past life, you had a very deep and thorough knowledge of Japanese. You lived in Japan for many lives. In this lifetime, you have no knowledge at all, consciously. When you begin to study Japanese, it seems like you'll never learn it or, let's say, it's as difficult for you as it is for any Westerner because the initial mindset that you have in this life has nothing to do with your past lives. It's what you've developed in this life, and it's trained in a non-Oriental based language. But if you're willing to be patient and learn the initial stages of Japanese, you will find that then suddenly you will jump ahead of most of your classmates in your knowledge and in your ability to learn Japanese. Because if you've known it in past lives, once you get through the basics—if you're patient and you regain a little bit of a mind-state—that will open up the doorway to past life knowledge.

The same is true of meditation. If you have meditated in other lives and you've practiced meditation and had spiritual insights, meditation is something you have to learn again, and you may be a little slow at it at first or just like anybody else. But if you persist, suddenly you'll reach a point where there'll be a breakthrough, and you will be astounded at how fast you'll progress. Suddenly you'll leap ahead of everyone else—not that it's competitive—if you've done a lot of practice in your past life because it's there to draw on. But you have to get to that place. And in each lifetime, that requires a certain amount of starting over. It doesn't just come, in most cases. Sometimes it does if a person is very, very, advanced. But usually we have to recapture the mind-state through a certain amount of mental work in this lifetime.

The same is true of composition of music, designing buildings, architecture, just about any past life skill. You have to pretty much start over. You have to pay your dues a little bit. But then you have the wealth of your past life knowledge to draw on. It just starts to come back to you. Anyone who is highly successful in a field in this life has probably been in it for many lifetimes, although they may not remember that. And once they were through the initial stages of learning, suddenly the brilliance, which was developed in other lives for a particular field or endeavor, returns to them.

Most people who practice meditation, if you are psychic at all, if you're drawn to meditation, if you're interested in spiritual matters, chances are you've done spiritual practice in other lives. And that spiritual practice has developed a certain mind-state, which is extremely similar to the mind-state necessary to be a successful computer programmer, systems analyst and AI expert. While you are at computer school or studying at the university, it may be difficult, or even more difficult for you if you just haven't done much work with your mind in this life. Once you get to a certain point, you'll find it's a very easy career to be successful in. You'll enjoy it thoroughly, and it's one of the most lucrative careers that there is, particularly, of course, if you get into designing products and things like that. There's no limit to it, to what you can do. And it's a very nice type of work because you're helping people process information, improve their lives.

Computers are tied in, and will only be more so in the future, with everything in our lives. And there's not much good software and there aren't a lot of good programmers, so it's a real service to humanity and the world to be a good programmer, and particularly if you design great products. You make it easier for everybody—everybody has less headaches and their businesses work better and their life is better and, of course, you get rich and develop your mind in a yogic way, in a Buddhist way. It's really the best of all possible worlds.

Naturally, you can practice or be involved in another career and advance your mind and your spiritual practice by being mindful, using your career to develop certain skills. But I have yet to see a career that is as similar, if not almost the same, in benefit as computer science is, to doing the advanced exercises. It's like being in a monastery. For eight hours a day, you're sitting there, seven hours a day, getting paid to do Buddhist exercises which are developing your mind. You do yoga all day and get paid for it. And it's fun. And it's exciting and it's lucrative and it's non-polluting. There's just nothing negative about it at all. And then, if you did a good morning meditation, you did computer science during the day and come home at night and do some more meditation, it's literally the same effect as doing practice all day. It puts you in a very high place.

Think of career as a vehicle. It doesn't have to be down time. And that's not just true of computer science. You could be sweeping the floor in a factory. Now you can just sweep the floor generally and gain nothing from it. Or you can sweep the floor intelligently. You can figure out the best way to sweep the floor, put your power into it, use it as a concentration exercise, be meditative about it. There are lots of things you can do with any task. You can stack firewood, fold your laundry, just organize your day.

Each time you do something in a clear, sharp and definitive way, you are using the higher mind. When you find a new way to do something, you've reached up into the intuitive levels of the astral, and you're creating on a higher level. There really is no down time in life if you use life properly. Most people don't do that, needless to say. They just stumble along. They want to get out of work as fast as they can. They want to make maximum money for minimum output, and that does not result in a happy life. There's no pride in your work, and work does not become an active force to advance your mental awareness into higher states. It doesn't compact you.

Let's say that you wanted to become an Olympic athlete, and you got a job that would develop your muscles the same way as an exercise program would. Naturally you'd have to pay for your life—you know you'd have to make your way in the world until the Olympic games came. Other people, perhaps they were subsidized, perhaps they had a scholarship or someone funded them, and they could just go train all day, but you didn't have that available to you. If instead, you got a job that was literally like training all day and you were getting paid at the same time, well, that would be the best of both worlds.

That's how a Buddhist uses career. And any career—being a doctor, being a lawyer, anything—can be used to advance yourself. The key is to have, to begin with, that sense, that possibility, that I'm working not just to get paid, but I'm working to advance myself; and that there's an inherent power in my career to advance myself spiritually. In other words, you shouldn't create a break, a syntactical break, in your mind between your career and your religious practice. If religious practice is something that you just do when you go to the temple or to the church for a couple of hours a week, that's not a lot of practice. The rest of the time is down time.

In the type of Buddhism that I teach, the career actually is the central point in practice since you spend perhaps two hours a day meditating, or maybe just an hour if you're new to meditation, a half an hour twice a day, and maybe 10 or 12 hours is devoted to the career between the commutation, the dressing, and going to school or the homework. That's a lot of time. If that time is turned into meditation, then you live in a high level of energy all the time. Your mind advances rapidly and you just dash along the path to more and more beautiful vistas. You experience deeper ecstasy through working, through going to school.

The central point, really, in the teaching I do is career, since we spend more time doing it and more energy is expended in it than anything else. Career becomes the most important item in our agenda to turn into a meditative form, a practice that makes us happy, that makes us wise, that makes us balanced, that develops our sense of humor, that develops our concentrative and meditative powers and then enables us to go into inter-dimensional realities that are bright and beautiful and empowering and, eventually of course, into enlightened stages of attention. Naturally, you can't really practice the yoga of career without practicing meditation by itself, sitting meditation, because you simply won't have the *kundalini* available to you. When you meditate in the morning and in the evening, you release *kundalini* energy. That energy, through the proper meditation upon the *chakras,* will enable you then to have the mental power to use your mind in your career in a new way each day.

Most people are operating out of repetition. In other words, if you come to work or school each day with the same mind-state, you probably can't get more out of it than you did yesterday. But if you meditate in the morning and you reach a mind-state you've never been in before, it'll stay with you throughout the day, and you'll be able to find new ways to utilize your career and your school work and just the routines of daily life—cooking, cleaning, getting the car serviced. There are millions of little opportunities out there to advance yourself. Everything in life is a pathway to enlightenment. But you have to have the personal power to see how to do it. You can know that as a theory, but it doesn't mean you can do it.

The personal power comes from meditating in the morning and meditating in the evening, and if you have an enlightened teacher, of course, receiving instruction and empowerments. But then if you combine that with a career like computer science, or just use whatever you have as a yoga—the career that you're in or the schoolwork that you're doing—you will find that your practice will not be in any way, shape, manner or form less powerful or less effective than a person who lives in a monastery. Not only can you be on a par with them, but you might even excel because practice in a monastery can get one-sided.

There are certain challenges that you face living in the world, certain difficult situations that you deal with that you don't deal with in a monastery. And sooner or later, the person in the monastery is going to have to overcome those things. Some people feel it's better to postpone it, solidify their practice, solidify their realizations and then take on the more difficult things. I like to just jump into everything at once because I think you've got to learn it anyway, and why not just tackle it to start with? If we're going running, let's do the uphill part of the run first, and then as we come back and we're a little more tired, we'll have the downhill to aid us, and we'll go with the flow of gravity. But when our power is up, when we're new to something, that's the time to tackle the rough stuff. It's kind of the fun. It's easier. We have more energy.

I think that it's better personally, I think one can advance faster, outside of the monastery. If you follow a tantric path, that is to say, a path in which you use the experiences of daily light, of daily life—that's a good Freudian slip—if you use the experiences of daily life to advance yourself, that's *tantra*. Tantra is the form of Buddhism and yoga in which not only is the *kundalini* released through *chakra* meditation, but daily experiences are used to advance oneself.

I think if you combine the experience of career and daily life with meditative practice and study with an enlightened teacher, I think while it's more difficult initially than going into the, you know, supportive environment of the monastery, you will progress faster. And then later in your life, once you've learned to deal with the world and the more complicated balancing issues of dealing, you know, with life in the physical and all the things that can happen that can jar you when you are outside of the monastery; once you've kind of gotten your rhythm for that, I think you'll progress much faster, and the second part of your incarnation will go much more smoothly—that's the downhill run. Whereas if you avoid that, which you do sometimes in the monastery, I think you'll find that while you'll learn certain things in a controlled environment, when you are out of that controlled environment, and you've gotten used to it, it can become debilitating to a certain degree.

It's not bad living in a monastery. I've done it many times, in many lives in teaching in them. Don't misunderstand me. But I think you can do a better job outside of the monastery if you have the necessary component parts. And I really think that computer science is one of those component parts. I can see no better way, if you don't live in a monastery, to practice because the mere practice of the art itself, of computer science, advances you, advances your mind in tandem with meditation. It's a very powerful, very potent way to free yourself materially and to advance yourself spiritually.

Career is yoga. Career is the Buddhist practice. I can think of nothing that is more so because it is what we do with our lives, and if we make that a spiritual thing, the thing that gives us energy and enlightenment, then enlightenment can't be very, very far off can it? Career is one of the pathways to enlightenment. And needless to say, I recommend computer science as the ultimate form of career for the reasons I have discussed.

CHAPTER TEN

MIRACLES

I like miracles. They inspire me. Miracles cause you to believe, have faith in the unseen, to look further into things, deeper into things. I like miracles. Miracles are the fun of enlightenment. When a teacher does a miracle—an enlightened teacher—and everyone sees it, they're astonished. And suddenly they have faith in what the teacher has to say about self-discovery and spirituality and enlightenment.

If you see a martial arts teacher dressed in their outfit, in their *gi* or in their black belt, it's impressive maybe—but if you watch them break a brick or several cement blocks with their hands and kick boards and things, it's very impressive. If you're looking for a martial arts teacher, you'll take them seriously because that's not an easy thing to do. Now, breaking bricks and boards is not necessarily the purpose of martial arts and it doesn't necessarily have a lot to do with fighting. But it makes a point, both in training in martial arts and, of course, for the student. The student sees the teacher do this and says, "Wow, this is incredible! This is a powerful person! This is a unique person who can do this!"

Miracles have a purpose. Miracles help people believe in

enlightenment. Enlightenment is something that in the beginning, and even sometimes in the intermediate phases of self-discovery, you're not aware of. You don't see it. It's not something that you're very conscious of. Enlightenment, initially, appears to be subtle. It's just out of the field of your vision. If you're meditating, if you're practicing every day, you don't necessarily see the changes that are taking place in your life because you're so close to them. You don't remember how limited your awareness field was six months ago or a year ago, let alone yesterday, before this morning's meditation. The real miracle, obviously, is the transformation of consciousness from limitation and pain, to enlightenment and ecstasy.

But in order to get to an appreciation, a belief, in order to inspire practice, teachers sometimes do miracles—or sometimes they just enjoy doing them. A miracle, a *siddha* power, is part and parcel of infinity. And I suppose you can use them to be egotistical and show off, but somebody enlightened wouldn't do that. They just have fun with it. It's an innocent play. An enlightened person lacks self-consciousness in the sense that there's no ego valuation for what they do. They just do things because it's fun, because it's beautiful or because that's how life flows through them.

It's inspiring when you see a miracle. Miracles cause you to believe. When the teacher does a miracle then you say, "Well, if they can do that, they must be unusually powerful, and there might be something to what they are saying about all this self-discovery and meditation stuff. It might be worth practicing."

Some people don't need miracles. They just believe. Or their life is painful, and they just want a change, and they are willing to try something—to try meditation, to try introspection—after trying many other things. Some people are just drawn without a particular reason. Maybe it's just past lives. And that inspires them—their karma compels them to follow the path to enlightenment. But, for many people, miracles are important. They're an important part of self-discovery, and some enlightened teachers do miracles to inspire people. Others do them simply because it's part of their job.

Now, I should point out that from the enlightened teacher's point of view, there aren't really any miracles other than the miracle of life itself. The use of the powers, of the *siddha* powers, is actually a very scientific application of occult energy through the occult body to do something specific.

If you went to a very rudimentary tribe that had never seen modern technology, then if you whipped out a little butane lighter and lit it, they would be astonished perhaps. They'd think you'd done a miracle. Somehow, just by moving your finger, you'd caused flame to sprout out of that little device. You know it's not a miracle. It's just a lighter. You know how it works. There's gas, there's a spark and the gas ignites and burns. The gas is stored in a little canister.

That's what the siddha powers are like. They're just an intelligent application of energy. It's like using a lighter. It's like doing anything technological. It's not a big deal. It's only a big deal to someone who doesn't understand what it is. Some of the more common siddha powers are, of course, physical healing, obviously empowerments and transformation of consciousness, physical healing to heal somebody of a disease they might have or an ailment, to bring them back from the brink of death to life just with pure energy, pure power. There are siddhas, of course, you know, that you've heard about—levitation, that kind of thing. There is the siddha of the *tumo,* to be able to create a lot of heat so that you're not cold even in a very cold environment—very useful in the caves of Tibet, by the way. There are a lot of different siddhas. You can read about them in mystical books.

I think, personally though, the most convincing miracle is the miracle of light that you see when you are with someone who is enlightened. When you visit an enlightened teacher, if you have the opportunity to meditate with them, if they sit in meditation, for a period of time you should close your eyes and meditate but you should also, once in a while, open your eyes and observe them. Look at the energy field around their body.

You will see—if they are enlightened and if you are not completely blocked up psychically—you'll see a number of emanations, a number of different lighting effects that are very beautiful to watch. You may see golden light, suffuse light, all around them. You may see them go into a kind of photo-negative that looks like everything reverses. You may see them dissolve in light. The light may grow so thick you can't even see them. You can't make out their body. You may see through them sometimes. Sometimes you can actually see right through them and see what's behind them. It depends on the state of attention that they're in.

But, as you watch an enlightened teacher, you will see this light after a while. Sometimes people come to an enlightened teacher and they don't see the light at all. They're just blocked up. Their mind is so caught up in the world of the senses and thought that they just simply can't let go and allow their occult eyes to see. They need to practice meditation for a while. But most people can see the light even the first time. Sometimes it's funny. They don't even know what they are seeing. It's so natural that it does not seem like it's unusual, and, well, I'll tell you a story.

When I meditate, people see manifestations of light when I go into *samadhi* and through the *samadhis*. And sometimes when I meditate, if I'm doing a public meditation, the energy of enlightenment is very clear—it's very high, it's very beautiful, and it's so clear that people don't realize that their attention has been elevated. When you're dealing with someone who is fully enlightened, the energy is so perfect, in a way of speaking, it's so shiny that you really don't know it's there.

I once had a judo teacher and he explained—he was telling us stories about great black belts and stuff—and he said there would be an opportunity—he had a fifth-degree black belt—to work with a sixth-degree black belt and get thrown by him. Now, immediately I was filled with terror. I was quite young at the time and I said, "Well gosh, wouldn't it be better to be thrown by a first-degree black belt and not by a sixth-degree black belt?" I assumed the sixth-degree black belt would sort of just mop you up all over the floor, and the first-degree black belt would be easier to deal with.

And he said, "No, no, no. It's much better to be thrown, if you are new, by a sixth-degree black belt, not by a first-degree black belt. A first-degree black belt is still new to the world of martial arts, and when they throw you, they might injure you. They can't see that you're a beginner. They don't have complete control yet. They might know you're a beginner, but they just don't have the control to get you to land correctly, to compensate for your lack of knowledge. A sixth-degree black belt, on the other hand, is so good at what they do that they'll place you on the ground just perfectly without injuring you. They'll be able to compensate for your lack of knowledge."

The same is true with teachers and with miracles. There are some teachers who just perform miracles. They can manifest things from the other world into this world. They're not necessarily enlightened. They have siddha powers. And they may even be spiritual. But the energy field around them, if you're a connoisseur of energy fields, is a little bit rough. There's an intensity to it that is not completely pure. If you're with someone who is truly enlightened, you know, a fully enlightened being—a *jivanmukta,* liberated soul—the light, the quality of the light is so clear, it's so perfect, that you don't really know that it's there until later.

In other words, their energy field when you're with them lifts you up, and you don't really recognize that you've been lifted up into altered states of attention, higher states of consciousness, until you come down later. It's so clean, it's so pure, it's so natural that there's no sense—they're so good at it that they throw you so perfectly into higher states of consciousness that you don't get injured. You don't even realize you're in a higher state of consciousness, it's so subtle, until later when you come down from that state of attention, and then suddenly you realize how high you were.

As I was saying, once I gave a talk at UCLA, and I was sitting there and I was meditating—this was many years ago—and there was a large crowd there. They had come to meditate with Rama. And I'm noted for colors and bright lights and special effects. Well, there's just a tremendous amount of visible light usually around me when I meditate. So I was—I got a kick out of it because I was mingling with the crowd afterwards. You know, I did the meditation, I gave a talk on enlightenment and Buddhism. And then afterwards, everyone was walking out, and sometimes I just like to walk with the crowd. I just like to be part of it and not necessarily be standoffish and go hide behind the curtain or anything. Sometimes I like to be standoffish. But that particular day, I just felt like walking with the crowd and just walking around.

I ended up walking behind two women, and they were having a

conversation. And it was interesting because they were talking about what they had seen, and one woman said to the other, "Oh, did you notice when he was surrounded by a red light?" And she said, "Oh yeah, I saw the red light. I saw the red light." Then the other one said, "Oh yes. And then there was the gold light, and then he just disappeared for a while. I couldn't see anything. There was just—the room went gold." She said, "Oh yeah, I saw that. And then did you see when everything went into reverse? Everything just kind of solarized." And she said, "Oh, yeah, I saw that." Then they chatted back and forth about what they had seen, and after they had this conversation, they said, "Well, what are we gonna do tomorrow night? Tomorrow night, let's go to the opera."

And I was listening to them converse, and it was interesting because they were so high they had no idea what they were saying. The things they were describing, we would class as miracles. To see someone manifest all the astral lights, to be surrounded by light, to have so much light emanating from their body, pulsing waves of gold light, that you couldn't even see anything else in the room—we would consider that a miracle. Again, it's the miracle of enlightenment. And these gals were up so high that they were talking about it as if it were any ordinary, everyday experience. They didn't even realize what they were saying because the energy of enlightenment had elevated their attention field so far that they were in a world in which that was normalcy, in which miracles were the norm.

And that's the world I live in. I live in a world where there is nothing but the miraculous. There is nothing but continuous light. There is nothing but continuous perfection. That's the world of enlightenment. Everything is subtle. Everything has a million sides. Everything is a manifestation of God. Everything is light. All beings are infinite. All things are perfect, in their own way. That's the greatest miracle, is to see things in the light of eternity.

The greatest miracle is silence. When everything is silent, when your mind becomes silent in meditation—by yourself or with a teacher—the world stops. Time stops. Life stops, as we know it, then something happens. We feel a feeling. We feel a longing. It kind of overtakes the spirit. We feel an eternality. Suddenly the world of busyness and times and places and spaces that occupies us, or the world of people and what we're doing tomorrow and what we're doing today and what we did yesterday, our plans, dreams and schemes fade away.

And we feel our eternality or we feel eternality. We feel the infinitude of being. And there's a longing. It's familiar. Suddenly this world, which has taken on such a significance, doesn't really matter. Suddenly it's just a memory. It's forgotten. And the spirit pines or longs for the world of light from which it came. It wants to return. There's a beautiful longing and that longing is fulfilled then by a suffusion of light. The longing causes something to happen. It causes the being to grow into light. The greatest miracle is the metaphysical process, in other words.

Yes, there are siddha powers. Yes, you can heal people, transform attention—there are lots of different things you can do. But they are just to inspire. You can flood the sky with light at night so you can't even see the stars. There are a lot of things you can do with the siddhas—open up the dimensional planes, manifest forces, beings, all kinds of things. But the greatest miracle is the light, the fact that the light comes to you when you have this longing. The spirit moves into light; it is light. It comes here for a while. I'm reminded by that Marvell poem, "On a Drop of Dew," where he compares the spirit to just a little drop of dew—that when the light of the sun falls upon it, it just, it quivers, and then it evaporates; it goes back into the air, into the ether.

Our spirit makes a journey. It wanders. And the miraculous is the world of enlightenment. Most people don't live in that world. The world appears to be solid to them. It's physical. It's just filled with their pain, their desires, their private ecstasies, their expectations—it's filled with *them*. "They" are the world. "They" are the universe, and nothing glows in that world. Everything is solid. The satisfactions are primarily physical—kind of basic. Nothing glows.

But when your consciousness expands, when you enter into the world of enlightenment, you're in a world—literally—of light. You don't have to be enlightened to have this experience. You just have to start the inner journey. You live in a world of light where nothing is solid. You travel about doing what you need to do each day, going through the doings of daily life, but your awareness field is luminous and it moves from dimension to dimension, back and forth from mortality to immortality. That's the miracle of enlightenment, of enlightened mind.

Otherwise you're caught in an empty house, in a box, in a place that's not happy. You're trapped inside *you.* And wherever you go, there you are. That's the rule. Wherever you travel to, you'll just find yourself in one form or another. And if you're jealous in one environment, you'll be jealous in another. If you're unhappy here, you'll probably be unhappy there. You take your internal baggage with you wherever you travel.

The miracle of enlightenment is that you let go of the baggage; you let go of the self. You take the self and let it dissolve in the white light of eternity. And then you live in that light. As you lessen the ego, as you dissolve the self a little more each day, you live in a greater condition of light, and the luminescence of that light is reality.

Reality is not this world. It's not the world as you perceive it. It's this world, but reality is the world as perceived through enlightenment. It's the same world, but it's not the same world. When you are in a condition of light everything is ecstatic, everything is joyous, everything is beautiful. Your attention field is subtle. And you are not assuming too much importance, if any at all. The ego is quiet. The mind is still. Your heart is happy, and then you go above all that to the fields of light.

In this world, in the world of solidity, there are experiences. I mean, let's face it, life for most people is a bad dream. Maybe you have a nice life, but most people on this earth don't. They live in pain, grabbing at what they can for pleasure. And as they grow old, they despair. The body that gave them pleasure now gives them pain. The life that gave them pleasure turns sour. Things don't work out the way you planned, for most people.

But if you meditate, then the real miracle is the transformation of your awareness field beyond the body. Beyond the body there is light, infinite light, and enlightenment—oceans of light, continents of light, universes of light. And you can experience those. Reality is a perfect light. And they free you from the limitations of this world, from the ugliness, from the unhappiness of limited perception. That's the greatest miracle.

I used to teach English as a Second Language at one time. And I was teaching at a college in New York one summer, teaching some summer classes. And I was teaching kids basically how to read, who were in college, but English was not their first language, Spanish was. And it was amazing to watch, to see what it was like when suddenly they could successfully read in English, which meant that they could fill out a job application, which meant that they could transact and get around without being embarrassed in this foreign culture. Suddenly it wasn't so foreign. And at the beginning of the summer they couldn't read real well or write real well in English, and at the end they could.

And to watch that transformation process was very exciting. To be able to participate in it was very exciting. And it's the same sense of the miraculous.

In other words, I think the most miraculous thing is learning. That's why I'm a teacher. That's why I was an English teacher. That's why I'm a teacher of enlightenment. It's why I am a teacher of martial arts and computer science and a few other things. Because when I teach, if I'm a good teacher, I get out of the way and let the student learn. You just guide them to what they need to know. And then you get to watch this amazing, amazing thing happen. You get to watch a life change. You get to watch the growth of an awareness field. The fact that we don't have to stay as we are, that we can improve our condition, incredibly, even just in the physical world, in terms of knowledge.

To watch a puppy grow into a dog or a child into an adult is an amazing thing. To watch someone go from the limitations of the physical plane where their awareness is bound up in the senses and thoughts and a very solidified sense of self and identity, and to watch them meditate and grow and develop and become not so physical—to watch light move into their life, to see the heaviness of their face change to lightness over a period of time, to see the person smiling, to see the radiant glow of inner light in the eyes, to watch them gain that silent knowledge that comes with inner study—that's the greatest miracle there is, from my point of view. That's why I'm a teacher.

I'm a teacher because teaching allows me to observe the universe at work. I like that change, that moment when wakefulness suddenly occurs, when something impossible becomes possible. When the universe is revealed to someone who thought they knew life, and they thought they knew what there was, and suddenly they realize they are only at the beginning—that the worlds of light, the planes of light, go on forever—that the experiences, the universes, of ecstasy, of intelligence, are perpetual.

I like the miraculous. It inspires me. And I choose teaching because it puts me more in touch with it. Like everyone else, I like a good miracle, in other words. It keeps me going. And the miracles that I see are the growth and development of my students, or the students of other teachers. I enjoy that. It refreshes and renews me and keeps my faith in the unseen very strong.

The greatest miracle is the miracle of wakefulness, to awaken from the dream of life and to see infinity everywhere, even in the finite, even in this world, in the simple doings of life—to be able to drive a car or mow the lawn, do your laundry, go for a run, go shopping, to take a shower—but in those activities to be in a field of light while you're performing them, and to see them as templates of all universes, of all realities. To be in thousands of states of mind simultaneously as you perform simple physical tasks gives you a reverence for life. You realize that there is nothing that is not perfect. There is nothing that is not miraculous. The simplest thing is a miracle if you see it truly because each of these outer manifestations of life is God, is the ultimate truth.

Buddhism leads you to this understanding. Buddhism leads you to the awareness that all things are holy, not just those who meditate and those who become enlightened. That would only be a partial understanding. The real miracle of life is that everything is holy—even the people who do the opposite of what you would consider to be spiritual are as miraculous. The dark has its own light, in other words.

In the beginning, we define what is spiritual and what is not, what is practice, what is not. But as you go on, you see that everybody and everything is an instrument of infinity. You see the miraculous in all things. That's the greatest miracle, of course, is that everything—not just the categories that you set up, but all things—are holy. All things are divine. And yet we pick and choose among them what's appropriate for us.

There are miracles, and they're inspiring. There are miracles of light. There are miracles of power—the ability to change things, affect things, to see and know things without being physically present. There are all kinds of siddhas. You can read about them in a book. But the greatest miracle is your journey into light. And if you're fortunate enough, you will gain the consciousness in this lifetime to see all things glow, to see that all things are really made up of light.

This solidity is not true. The apparent solidity is the delusion of the senses and of the self. Everything is made up of infinite, intelligent light. And if you look into anything, you can follow that light back to its source, which is everywhere and nowhere, which is nirvana, which is enlightenment.

Chapter Eleven

Intermediate Meditation

We find ourselves in the world. We're born here. We don't know why. We look around and we see life. We feel it. Sometimes it hurts. Sometimes it's pleasurable. Sometimes it's boring. Sometimes it's exciting. Sometimes it's frightening. Sometimes it's beautiful beyond comprehension.

Our bodies grow and develop. Our mind develops. We have experiences. And then something more happens for some people, and they begin to develop spiritually. It's an ache at first, a longing, a feeling for another time, another place, another condition. We want more. Or less.

We can feel the earth on a sunny day, feel the heat on a rainy day, the wetness, the wind. In the city, we hear the traffic, the noises; in the country, the sounds of the forest. We can make love, make money, go to work, feel fatigue, be excited. These are the things people do. One day melts into the next. And all you have for the days that you've gone through are memories, for the days that have not yet occurred, anticipations.

All that truly exists is this moment. This moment you're

experiencing now.

Yoga is a science. It's the science of consciousness. It suggests that there's more, or less—that outside of what you experience there are other realms, other dimensions that go on forever. They're just beyond the portals of your vision. There are dimensions of light, perfect light, on the other side of sense experience and mental experience. There are dimensions of ecstasy, worlds where time does not exist, and there's nirvana, the central nexus from which all this comes, the creator, enlightenment.

Meditation is traveling. It's a journey. It's a process by which we go from here to there with our minds. We see that the mind is infinite. It's not relegated to the brain or to thought or to emotion. It's made up of an endless series of realities that stretch on into infinity. You can come to know these realities. You can experience them directly yourself. This is the essence of Buddhism. And this process is the gaining of self-knowledge, of the awareness of life or its many awarenesses.

I'm a teacher of meditation. I've been teaching meditation for a while—many, many lifetimes. I'm also a student of meditation. There's always something new to learn. And I've observed a very interesting thing—that most people who meditate don't meditate. They think they're meditating, but they're not really meditating.

Meditation is concentration in the beginning. It's a focus. Then, in the intermediate stage, it's an opening, a deepening of one's awareness but with a focus towards the planes of light. In intermediate meditation, you're touching light more deeply than in introductory meditation. In advanced meditation, you become light. You transcend self, ego, time, space, dimensionality. You merge with the clear light of reality, you enter *samadhi,* and you go beyond this world.

Your ideas, your feelings, your needs, your wants, your loves, your hates, your ups, your downs—you go beyond it all and you become God. You become nirvana. You become enlightenment, for a while, for a timeless time. You merge with the ecstasy of the clear light of reality. And it changes you. It remakes you. It reforms you. It shifts you, and then you're that.

Your awareness returns to the world brighter, different, less solidified. And repeating this process endlessly or in many years and many lifetimes eventually will culminate in the experience of enlightenment where you will always be in a state of light, a condition of limitless awareness. And it goes on forever. As Bilbo tells us in his story in *The Hobbit,* his little song he sings, the road leads on forever. That's the good news. There's no end to enlightenment. There's no end to incarnation. There's no end to infinity.

And then there's the world of pain and discouragement and frustration that most people live in, where they watch their bodies age and their hopes fade, and the things they believe and love are destroyed. There are moments. Good moments. But there are a lot of bad moments, if we're going to be real about what human life is for most people.

People who meditate seek good moments forever. They know that there are other worlds beyond this world. They feel it. It's true. It's not imagination because it's something that you can experience directly when you sit to meditate. I experience those worlds when I meditate, and I teach others to experience them. But as I said before—it's amazing—I've observed that a lot of people who profess to meditate don't meditate. They sit, they engage themselves in some kind of concentrative practice, but it's not what I would call meditation because they allow too many impressions into their mind. So our topic is intermediate meditation.

In introductory meditation, you learn to focus on the three chakras—the navel chakra, the chest chakra and the third eye, between the eyebrows and a little above. These are the three primary doorways that take in the three primary meridians of power, balance and wisdom. You learn to sit for 15 minutes, half an hour or 45 minutes, maybe even an hour, and focus in turn on these three chakras. If you're a student of mine, of course, you meditate to music that I've composed, and it's played by some of my students in our group, Zazen. Music that comes out of higher dimensions, that's extremely pure, and if you focus on it during meditation, it will make the mind quiet. And it ensures that you will touch worlds of light and brightness, that you'll be headed in the right direction, as opposed to the wrong direction. It also acts as an auric block—the energy in it—to block out the billions and billions of auras from the people who live on this planet, so that you can just sit in your own aura and then direct your mind to infinity and move from this world to infinity, experience the ecstasy of infinity and come back, better for your journey, more conscious, happier, wiser, hopefully sillier.

Now that's meditation as I've come to know it; as it was taught to me by my teachers over many, many lives, and as I teach it. It's always the same, yet it's always new. But the process involves stopping thought—first slowing it down, detaching yourself from it, but eventually stopping thought and then directing yourself towards light.

This is the key—directing yourself towards light, not towards other people, not towards places, things, but towards light. What is light? What is this light I talk of? Light is awareness—awareness without mental modifications. If you can stop your thoughts and allow nothing else into your mind, you will experience light. If you stop your thoughts just for five minutes, you'll experience a very deep light. That light is on the other side of the sense perceptions—seeing, tasting, smelling, touching, feeling. Just on the other side of sense perceptions is a beautiful, perfect light. It's so close to us. It's always around us, yet we're relatively unaware of it because we're distracted by the images of life, by the world of physicality.

There's nothing wrong with the world of physicality. There's nothing wrong with existence. It's perfect. But it's terribly transient. Your body—its cells, its longings, its wants—are terribly transient.

These things don't last very long, and very often they leave a great deal of pain and frustration in their wake.

Enlightenment is the alternative—to enter into a condition of perfect light, to have complete peace and stillness in your mind, to not be frustrated when things don't go your way, to go a different way, different than the people of this world. People of this world, who knows where they're going? Every day, they're going someplace else.

I see them driving cars, winding down the streets. I don't know where these people think they're going. They're all going to the local funeral home, that's about it. And between where they are today and this local funeral home, they're going to have experiences which are going to be forgotten really fast. I love it.

There's a sign—I'm sure you've seen something similar on the highway—near where I live, and it's from my local funeral home, and it says the name of the funeral home, then it says in huge letters, "Slow down! Enjoy Life!" Now really, that's the essence of it. Then it says, you know, local funeral home.

That's it, isn't it? Slow down. Enjoy life. Chill out. You know, it's tough to slow down if your mind is going a million miles a second. It's tough to slow down if you think what these people do here matters. I mean, you need a form of government; you need a place to live, you need something to eat, you need some entertainment, yeah, OK. But what else do you need? What these people do here is obviously not working. They're unhappy. They sit in their commuter traffic hour after hour, or they make the earth a toxic waste dump. They've got lots of theories, lots of books, lots of sciences—I've read a lot of those books. And you know most of them are pretty unhappy.

There's an alternative. And it's an old alternative. It's not for everybody. It's only for people who are smart. Limited market. It's enlightenment—to become aware that there's more to life than television, to stretch your mind and touch infinity, to feel eternity around you. Not as an idea, not as a nice intellectualization, but to really feel it; not to be a religious fanatic who's strung out on some weird idea of salvation to the exclusion of common sense—I'm not talking about that.

The real religious experience is the experience of life, but to experience life, not as an ideation, not as a bunch of thoughts that are whipping around in your head and explosive emotions that are out of control, desires that are endless and unrealistic, frustrations that just don't matter. If we really come down to it, what's the purpose of life? To be happy. What else could it be? And happiness does not come from other people. It doesn't come from places. It doesn't come from things. It's inside your own mind. All happiness is inside your own mind. Chances are, you have not discovered that yet. That's an interesting phrase, but chances are, you haven't experienced it.

Intermediate meditation is about experiencing the happiness that's inside your mind. If you're sitting, practicing meditation on a daily basis and you are not experiencing a greater happiness every day, then you're certainly not meditating.

It's not hard to do, to be happy. It's not hard to experience that happiness, but you must meditate correctly. And as I said before, I observe many people who say they're meditating, but I sure don't see them meditating. They sit and they touch a lot of people, places and things psychically, but they sure don't meditate.

To understand what I mean by this, let's consider what meditation is and is not. When you sit to meditate, you become very psychic. You're focusing on the navel center, chest center, third eye, something like that. You're listening to perhaps music. Or you might be doing a different type of meditation, another type, that another teacher might teach—you know, focusing on the breath, focusing on posture; the eyes might be open, focusing on a yantra.

I mean, there are different ways to meditate. They're all leading to the same place. They're all ways of focusing your attention, withdrawing it from the senses so instead of looking through your physical eyes or through these things, you're bringing your awareness into one place and then you're directing it towards unlimited light, towards the planes of light. There are other planes, there are planes that are not light, there are planes that are shadowy. But that's not our interest in meditation. We want brightness. We want ecstasy, brilliance beyond comprehension, to merge with that ecstasy of life and to go into the stillness and dissolve the ego; to be the totality, to be all things. Not just to gain power over things—how infantile. If you even care about things, that means they have power over you.

Not only to be at peace, but to be a bright field of light—intelligent, endless light—that which makes the universe. That's what we are. But you've got to get to that deeper part of yourself, to that deeper part of life. So the mind must be made calm and still like a lake without any ripples, and then it's aimed at the sky, at the brightness, at infinity, at that infinitude of being that stretches out endlessly in every direction forever.

Intermediate meditation is sitting, the way I teach it, focusing on a chakra, let's say an hour meditation session—20 minutes on the navel center, 20 minutes on the chest center, 20 minutes on the third eye. Just 60 minutes—but each of those 60 minutes divided into the three 20-minute units must be directed towards light. Because when you meditate, particularly once you've been doing it for a while, your meditation is a very powerful time. Very powerful. And you're very psychic. When thought slows down, when you're focusing on these chakras, you become very psychic. And it is most important during that period of time from one minute to the next not to allow your attention, your mind, to wander towards anything but four primary areas of focus.

You can focus on the chakra to the exclusion of everything else. You can focus on your teacher to the exclusion of anything else, if you have an enlightened teacher. You can focus on music, if you're listening to enlightened music, to the exclusion of everything else, or you can focus on light to the exclusion of everything else.

Let me give you a little template here of what I mean. If you're sitting to meditate—now let's say the first third of the meditation, you're going to spend focused on the area of the navel, the power center, to bring up raw power. The second section, you're going to bring it up to the chest center, focus there, and that raw power will transmute when it gets up there into love, into an ecstasy of oneness. And then we're going to go up to the third eye, and once it's been transmuted, and bring it up higher on the chakra scale into wisdom, into knowledge, into pure and perfect seeing of worlds of light and experiencing. That's our plan.

Let's start down in the navel center. You've got 20 minutes—15 minutes or 10 if you're just meditating for 30 minutes or 45 minutes—but let's say you're doing the hour. You're down there for 20 minutes in the world of power. Now for that 20 minutes, you have to keep your mind on light. If your mind does not focus on light, then whatever it focuses on, because you're in a highly psychic state, you're going to take through your aura in a way that you would normally take almost nothing through your aura.

Normally your aura is like an immune system. It keeps things out. But in meditation, that immune system is removed, consciously. We want it removed. Because not only does it block out things that are negative, but it also blocks out things that are positive. We're going to consciously move it to the side for a period of time and then, of course, during that period of time, by having a complete focus on light, brightness, spiritual oneness, God, infinity, eternity. You know, silly things. By doing that, then we are going to bring that into our aura. We are going to touch it psychically, and it's going to touch us. We're going to merge with it. We have to move the protective aura aside for a time to do that. Then, at the end of meditation, the protective aura will be even stronger because we're energized, and it will block out everything negative. And we've filled ourselves up with so much light, that we're set. We're satisfied, so to speak. We've come back from our journey, and now we've closed the door.

It's not—you know, some people have a kind of paranoid feeling. They say, "Well, when you meditate, if you're outside of your body, can something get in your body?" No, this is nonsense. I'm talking about keeping your awareness pure. You don't leave the body—that's a way of talking. You become a little less aware of the physical side of your being because you become more aware of the spiritual side of your being. Nothing's going to get in. You're there. But in an intensified period of focus, when your mind is locking onto something, it's most important that it only lock onto something bright, beautiful and perfect.

Now when a lot of people meditate, what they do is, the whole time they're there, they're thinking about other people, sometimes even psychically talking to them, telepathically. This is a terrible mistake. If you do this, stop. Or if you're new to meditation, make sure you never start. Because during the period of meditation, when you drop that auric immune system shield, if you focus on another person, if you feel different people, you take their energy in your body completely. You completely absorb their energy, and you experience a kind of a psychic overload. All their thoughts, their desires, their impressions, their restlessness, their unhappiness, their confusions—all enter you. If you were to think of 10 or 15 people in a row, even for a few moments each, during meditation, you're in such a psychic state, it's so powerful, that each of those person's minds will enter your mind, and you'll just be completely gummed up psychically.

In other words, in meditation, what you're trying to do is simply get rid of your own junk. You're trying to move all the confusion out of your mind, all of the heaviness, the emotional upsets, the impressions that you've picked up since your last meditation. It's kind of like taking a shower, where you're just going to wash all the dirt off that you've picked up since your last shower and be clean. Then from there, we can move into the world of light.

In meditation, if you start picking up other people's impressions while you're meditating, then instead of clearing yourself, you're just going to completely glom yourself up to the point where there's going to be no meditation. You're going to end the period of meditation in a much lower state—lower vibratory state—than when you started. Now a lot of people do that, and they get very dissociated because they sit and they think of other people. Or they focus on things that vibrate very slowly, during meditation. And because you're in such a highly sensitized state during meditation, because you're so open, then you just make yourself really sick, psychically.

The way to avoid this is to have things to focus on during meditation. And as I said, there are four things you can really focus on that are very healthy. You might come up with something else, but these are four that are for sure. You can focus on a chakra, to the exclusion of everything else. You can focus on your teacher to the exclusion of everything else, if you have an enlightened teacher. You can focus on enlightened music or you can focus on light itself.

Now let's get basic. The first 20 minutes of your meditation session, if you're meditating for an hour, sit down, put on a meditation album. I have three meditation albums at the moment. The *Enlightenment* album is for morning meditation, *Canyons of Light* is for evening meditation and *Samadhi* can be used for morning or evening.

Let's say it's morning and you have the *Enlightenment* album on. You just got up, took a shower, drank some tea or coffee, if you need that to wake up—if not, water or juice will do. You're feeling pretty good, a little tired. Sit down, sit in a cross-legged position, sit up nice and straight. Focus on the navel center.

Now this is intermediate meditation, so you're used to doing this. You've been doing this for a few months or maybe even a year. It's no longer a big deal to sit down, focus on the navel, the chest center, the third eye. You've gotten used to that. You've met me, perhaps, an enlightened teacher, or maybe some other teachers, so you've experienced to a certain extent the feelings of meditation. If you've been with some enlightened teachers while they've meditated, just being with them, their aura expands you, and you've gotten a sense of what meditation is—that feeling of timelessness, of perfect beauty, of endless awareness.

You plop on down, meditate—sit on down, meditate—close your eyes, focus on the navel center. You've got 20 minutes; the music is on. Now, the key issue is, what are you going to do during that 20 minutes as you focus? OK, well great, what is focus? That means that you're going to bring your attention to the area of the navel or a couple of inches below. You're going to feel that area. Not just casually, or vaguely, but you have to hold your mind there. It's like doing pushups. I mean, it's a complete focus. You're going to hold your mind on the area of the navel to the exclusion of everything else. There's a chakra, an energy center there, and it doesn't activate unless you're focusing intensively.

You focus your attention around the navel area. You feel that spot. Visualize it. Do whatever it takes. Once you're there, just keep focusing. When thoughts come in and out of your mind, you pay no attention. Pictures, thoughts of people, feelings, you don't pay any attention. You just stay right on that spot! You can probably only focus on that spot for two or three minutes at a time, unless you're a very strong meditator. It's hard to keep your focus there.

Now when I say "focus," I mean to the exclusion of everything else. It's so intense that there are no thoughts. There are no feelings. You're not aware of anything else. Usually you can only do that in short bursts in the beginning, the beginning being the first, you know, few hundred incarnations of practice.

What do you do?

Well, most people might—if they focus intensively to begin with—after a few minutes they'll relax, they'll stop, and their mind will drift. Now they're in a highly charged psychic state and they're going to absorb whatever they think of, and it's going to screw up their meditation. There are alternatives. You're sitting, listening to enlightened music. So after focusing as hard as you can on the navel center, and when you simply can't do it any more, accept that, don't fake it. Now, shift your focus. Keep a general feeling of the navel center, that is to say, kind of feel that area of your body—always keep part of your attention there during the first 20 minutes. But now focus on the music.

Now when I say focus on the music, I don't mean listen to it as if it's a song on the radio that you sort of hear, sort of don't, while you think of other things—your mind drifts, you imagine people, you imagine places, you imagine things, you think about tomorrow, you remember yesterday—all that sort of nonsense. Don't do that. Absolutely not. Bring your attention to the music. Listen to every note.

Go into every feeling. Focus on it so you don't hear anything else. Now you're doing a hearing, a listening meditation. Focus completely till there's nothing but that pure and perfect sound.

Now that you've done that as long as you can, maybe three, four minutes, maybe one song—but you listen to it perfectly—when you're doing that psychically, just like with a chakra, you're entering the chakra, you're entering this music. This music is composed in other dimensions. That's where I go to compose it. Then it's brought here into this world from the planes of light. And it's played by some of my students. Then I go through the music that they've played—with my aura—and wash out anything impure aurically, so there's only light in the music. It's perfect music on an auric level.

Focus on the music. Go into it. Meaning, feel where it's coming from and travel with it. Travel to those emotive places that are described in musical alliteration through the songs. When you can't do that anymore, be real about it. Now you've saturated yourself that way, now focus on, perhaps, your teacher, if you have a teacher who's enlightened, a teacher who is no longer in the body, but they were enlightened—Ramakrishna, somebody like that. Or if I'm your teacher, you think of your teacher. Now you have to be careful when you do this because the teacher's aura is very powerful. But first you have to make sure you're even connecting with the teacher's aura.

If, for example, you've only seen your teacher with hundreds of other people around and you've never had a moment with them, a private moment, you might be making a mistake. Because when you sit with a lot of people and your teacher is present, you might not be feeling much of the teacher's aura; you may be feeling simply the auras and impressions of all the people who were there to see the teacher. You may begin to associate that with how the teacher feels, but maybe that's not the case. You have to get a sense of what it feels like. Now, listening to me on this tape, if you listen very intensely, you can feel the emptiness, the perfect emptiness of my mind. There are no thoughts. There are no impressions. There's only light, the light of enlightenment. It's perfect. It's pure. It's pristine. It's endless.

I meditate and have meditated very, very hard so that there's nothing but light. There's no human confusion. There's only perfect light. Now feel that as we pause for a moment—for a moment, I will meditate here—and feel this light.

(Silent pause.)

Now, that's the emptiness. That's the light. It comes in endless forms. If you have had a personal experience with me as a teacher, a moment when we were alone, and you've felt that perfect light, or you were out in the desert or whatever, but it's a moment that definitely is not associated with other people's minds, then you can focus on that, or you can focus on just a moment like we just had together. In other words, it's a tuning fork. It's a *mantra*. It's a key. It's a template to other universes. But it has to be pure.

Some people see teachers, and they associate the feelings of the other students who are present with the teacher. And so when they sit to meditate and they imagine their teacher, they're really imagining all those people who were there, and psychically they connect, at the moment they imagine them, with all those hundreds of minds wherever they happen to be today. They pull all that stuff in, and they get completely dissociated and they don't key to the teacher at all. So if you're going to focus on a teacher, it has to be done properly. You have to be focused very much on the teacher and not peripheral vibrations that might have been around them, or it will totally screw up your meditation.

There is always a sense of being alone, a beautiful aloneness to meditating. Not a *loneliness,* but a beautiful *aloneness.* You're sitting in the middle of infinity or some far-flung corner, and you are merging with it. It's an alone feeling. You can't have other people there. If other people come to you psychically in meditation, push them away. Don't see their faces. Don't think of their minds. Push them away with your power. It has to be alone.

Only alone can you go into eternity. Only alone can you feel that transcendental light. Only alone will it purify you and perfect you. It is not a shared experience because if it's shared, you're down in duality. You're not up there. You're down in the world of bonding realities where there are multiple minds and multiple forms and multiple confusions. And that is not meditation.

Meditation is a pure experience. By pure, we mean undiluted. It is not something that you can share with others. It is something that you experience alone. You by yourself were born into this world. You may have come through your mother's body, but you have nothing to do with her other than that. Your spirit is ageless, timeless and immortal. That spirit may have taken physical form and come through a physical body, but you come into the world alone and when you die, you will die alone, even if you die in the company of another person, if you both died together. Yet each in your own mind you are alone, and you will leave this world alone and go to the next world alone.

We are alone. It is our condition as perceivers. We can experience others, and others are a reflection of the universal mind, yes, and that's fun, of course. But the period of meditation is a time when we go back to the source. We go back to what we were before we were born. We go back into essence. We have lots of time in substance. But we need to renew ourselves. We need to regain our purpose, to discover who we are. These aren't things you can express in words. They're feelings, knowings, intuitions that you can experience when you meditate. Meditation is quite a complicated thing. It's a return to the source. We're going back into the light, into the perfection, into the unborn, uncreated state. And as long as we can sustain ourselves in that state, we will be renewed, transformed. All our pain will be taken away, our frustration, all of the aggregates that we pick up in the human plane, in this, you know, dimensional reality, will be washed away, and we will be spirit, pure spirit, pure light, pure love, pure ecstasy. Then we can come back into this world and address the tasks of our life brightly and happily.

Our work, our play, school, relationships—wherever our karma takes us—we can live fully because we're not confused. We know that we're infinite spirit. We know that we can't die. We can go through the experience of death, but we see in meditation that our experiences are endless, that we're an endless, eternal spirit. Not as a thought or an idea you read in a book. You had the experience yourself. Every day.

And as you get better at meditating, you have that experience more strongly, more profoundly and it changes everything for you. But you have to stay to the center, if this is the sort of thing you like. You've got to go for it. Or you can drift. You can meditate once in a while and just have a lot of other experiences. Then you're in what we call the *samsara,* the world of illusions, the world of human experiences—the emotions, the feelings, the passions, the loves, the hates, you know, all that good stuff. You're in that world and you're moving around in it. But you will not be in the *transcendental reality.* That is to say, you're in the world of time and space and dimensionality, and you must accept the conditions of that world. You have no choice.

On the other hand, if you meditate, you can experience that world, but you can experience the other world and the far-flung eternities and dimensions, and you're not stuck in any one of them. If the physical world gets to be problematic, you can easily slip off into worlds of brightness and spirit and reinterpret your experiences in the physical world and not know suffering and pain from them. You decide.

You don't have to meditate. It's not necessary. You don't have to practice self-discovery and Buddhism. It's not necessary. You can just go live. You should only experience ecstasy when you meditate, and you should only practice self-discovery if you have really had it with the human world. If you feel that there's a bright, beautiful world out there with nothing but wonderful experiences every day, you don't need to meditate, I guess you're there. Either that, or you need a good psychiatrist.

On the other hand, if you're like most of us who have lived a little bit, maybe you're a little wiser and you realize that life is complicated. It has its good moments, it has its bad moments, it has its ups, it has its downs, its ins and its outs. And there's usually a lot more pain than pleasure and a lot more unhappiness than happiness. Otherwise, you've been watching too many TV commercials and too many sitcoms. Get real. Life is heavy. It's difficult. It's complex, even for the wise. Examine your experience of the incarnation so far and realistically add up the moments of happiness and unhappiness, and you tell me. Oh somewhat vaguely nobly born, you tell me, what has it been like for you?

People who are drawn to meditation have had lots of incarnations in the world of experience, and we know the score. We know that experience is great, but it's not enough. We have gone around the loop enough times. You know, it's like relationships. You start a relationship with someone and everything is wonderful in the beginning and then it's not. You might work it out. It might have more moments that are positive than negative. But only people who haven't had relationships think that they're just always wonderful and, you know, carefree. We're in the world of Stayfree MiniPads where everything is perfect all the time. I'm afraid not.

Grow up. Get a life. Life is pain, and anybody who tells you something other than that is trying to sell you something. Absolutely. Life in the physical world. But then there's ecstasy, the ecstasy of enlightenment. But if you're going to experience that and it's not just going to be a phrase, you've got to work during meditation. So, back to the navel center!

In the navel center, you're focusing on the chakra as long as you can, and then maybe focusing on music as long as you can, then the teacher—but the teacher in a pure way, not just the feelings of hundreds of people who might have been there when you saw your teacher. Because whatever you focus on during meditation, you psychically actually travel to and touch. It's not just a thought. You might think of a person in your normal waking consciousness and not necessarily touch them very deeply. But in meditation, when you think of somebody, you actually go into their aura at that moment and you pull it into your aura. That's the issue. It's most important to keep your meditation pristine, unalloyed.

Now after you focus on the teacher as long as you can, well, then try pure light. Just feel or imagine an infinite field of white, bright, perfect light or any color you choose, and just go into it. Hold the image in your mind very strongly. Then once you can't do that anymore, if your time for that chakra is not up, go back to the chakra. In other words, have a number of things you can move your mind to, each of which is bright and perfect, that connects you with light—not human aura or anything lesser—during the experience of meditation.

It's not enough to just say, "Well, I'm going to sit down and focus on a chakra for 20 minutes. And then the next chakra, and then the next chakra, and that's an hour of meditation." You're not going to meditate. You're going to drift all over the place in a highly empowered state and touch many, many auras and pick up a lot of negativity. You must have a number of focuses, or call them shields, if you will, during the experience of meditation. Because you're in an empowered state, and let's be realistic—unless you have total control over the mind, the mind wanders. But you can't let it wander.

So every time your mind moves toward something, don't be uptight, don't be afraid, just, you know, that you're going to get sick or something, or pick up too much aura—that'll only happen if you don't then move the mind. And of course, the fun part is you're developing a new neural track. You get better at this. It becomes a habituation, a habit. And good habits are as hard to break as bad habits.

Try and break a good habit sometime. It's not easy—if you have some good habits. If you have good posture, try and slouch. It doesn't come naturally. If you have good habits, you know, they're your friends. And you can develop a positive good habit, which is called meditation—meditating properly. And it'll take about a week or two to get the track laid well. And if you've been doing it incorrectly for years, then it will take a month or two to redo it.

The real issue is to use the full power of your concentration. If you find that you're drifting and drifting, and you can't do an hour meditation, then just do a half an hour meditation. But it has to be done intensively. Better to do the hour, if you can. I think you can, if you do it in small, incremental modules. That's the method that I think is preferred. As I've suggested, now that we've moved up to the heart, you know, the chest chakra, perhaps what you'll do here is start with the chakra, focus on it as long as you can, as hard as you can. And of course, you pick up energy doing this—makes everything brighter. Now focus on the music for a few minutes. Now focus on your teacher for a few minutes. Now focus on light. Then go back to the chakra—or in any order your prefer.

Focus on something bright and beautiful. But you must keep your mind occupied at every moment with that which is bright and beautiful. If you do, then there will be nothing else. There won't be people, places or things, the future or the past in your mind.

You can't just sit in emptiness. Even the enlightened don't sit in emptiness. We call it emptiness, but we move our mind into a world of light. Meditation is not emptiness. That's a way of trying to talk about something that is impossible to put into words. It's not that it's empty; it's a world of fullness, if anything. Meditation, in other words, is not really thinking of nothing. In the beginning, it's just replacement thinking. Instead of having the usual negative things that kind of wander around in your mind, or limited things, certainly—people, places, things, you know, past, future, emotion, in most cases—you are replacing those things with very bright images. Now those bright images—when you're in an empowered state, in a highly psychic state—are not just images. They're doorways.

Whatever you focus on, you become. That's the key line, you know. Meditation is the bow and concentration is the arrow. Whatever you focus on, you become, particularly during that highly charged state when you let go of that auric immune shield intentionally because you want to go beyond it into pure brightness, into pure light. But you must be very, very careful not to allow other images to come into your mind. Just *fwak* them right out. It's like playing a great video game. Every time another image comes in your mind, just push it out. Don't focus on it a lot when you push it out, or you'll connect with it.

The way you push it out is by refocusing onto something bright. And this is the good habit you will develop. You're sitting there meditating, and every moment you're focusing on either a chakra, the music, light, or your teacher or something else that will connect you with the dimensions of light. And every time something else comes in your mind for a moment—you think of a person, an experience, whatever it is—you consciously must pull your mind back from that image by substituting an image of brightness. If you try to sit in emptiness, you're creating a vacuum. It'll be filled by something. It'll be filled by thoughts and images from your memory or just things that you're feeling psychically. Uh-uh. You have to substitute something and refocus.

Meditation, in other words, is a refocusing—in the intermediate stage—on symbols. And through these symbols, you will come to know your own mind. It's not emptiness. We're using symbols, doorways to step from here to there—from one world to another, from darkness to light, from death to immortality.

Think of meditation then, on the intermediate level, as a substitution. We're substituting a bright thought for a dark thought, a happy moment for a sad moment, an infinite feeling for a finite feeling, a cosmic awareness for a mundane awareness. And what you're doing is learning to retrain your mind. For one hour, or half an hour, 45 minutes, when you sit to meditate, you're retraining the way your mind works. You've never trained it; it just sort of happened growing up. Now you're actually training the mind to focus on brightness to the exclusion of all other things.

If you do this during the period of meditation, then it will more readily occur the rest of the time—when you're not sitting in a postured meditation—as you go through the day and the evening. You're setting up a template, a good habit. When you first get up, and hopefully again in the evening, you do another equal period of meditation, and you're pulling up power and energy to allow yourself to do all kinds of things and use more of the mind and be in multiple dimensions and all that good stuff. Of course.

But what you're doing is re-routing the way you perceive. You're taking a limited perception—which is the sense world and the mental world and the emotional world, which is what most people have—and you're expanding your perceptual ranges so that you can perceive more ranges, greater ranges, all of the time, not just during the period of meditation. And of course, you will experience the normal ranges of perceptions, actually with a lot more clarity and depth because your mind will be clear and sharp and it will have a lot of energy and all the junk will be out of it. Your physical tasking will be tighter and brighter. And of course, you'll be happy.

So what have we learned thus far? In other words, hopefully we're redefining, or perhaps defining meditation for you for the first time. What have we learned? We've learned, essentially, that meditation—intermediate meditation—is a refocusing, a retraining of the mind. To just think that you're going to do what you did in introductory meditation for a longer period of time is incorrect. You're not just going to plop yourself down to meditate and focus on a chakra, meaning once in a while you'll focus on it, most of the time you'll drift all over the place. That's introductory meditation. You're just getting used to sitting, focusing; sometimes you feel some energy;

sometimes you don't.

What we have learned is that intermediate meditation is the use of symbols, not abstractions. A symbol is something alive. It's a connector. It's a hyphen between one reality and another. We're in one room. We have to go to another room. We need a doorway to go through. We open the door. We pass through, and we're in another reality. These symbols are doorways to other realities. Focusing on an enlightened teacher is a doorway. It's not a person. We're focusing on the light that passes through them. But our mind is holding the physical image of the person. As we hold that image, our psyche is connecting with the light within them, then we are moving not to them but through them into that field of light, into the planes of light that stretch on forever, and eventually to nirvana.

The *chakra* is a doorway. When you hold on the navel center, it's the chakra leading you to the planes of power. When you focus on the chest center, it's leading you to the planes of emotive feeling, of spiritual oneness, of ecstasy and happiness. When you're focusing on the third eye, you're going to the planes of knowledge and vision. These are doorways that lead you to these other dimensions. But you have to focus on them completely to the exclusion of everything else. You can't just vaguely hold onto them. Nothing will happen. Or worse yet, you will empower yourself to a degree, become highly clairvoyant, and then, if you allow other images—particularly of people, places and things—to pass through your mind during that state, you will pull in all those other auras, and you will be much more confused and much more dissociated than you were prior to your meditation experience.

Intermediate meditation is learning to use the mind in a new way. And eventually we will develop a habit, a good habit that we will use not only during the period of meditation but 24 hours a day. The answer is not to try and sit in emptiness and just have the good intention that you're going to hold your mind in a perfect state. Nonsense. Get real. Get a life. That's not going to happen.

Good intentions are not enough. You have to know what you're doing. You need the techniques. By having a number of symbols, doorways that you can focus on from one moment to the next, there will never be a gap during the period of meditation. At times you may go through the doorways and enter into light. Then there's only light in the mind, there's no thought, there's no images, there's no psychic connection with other people, places, things, times, or all that sort of stuff—beings, whatever. So then, naturally, that's fine.

If you're in light, the only time you then have to refocus is when the light fades, gravity pulls you back to the mind and suddenly the images are coming up of the world again. So then, jam ahead. Focus on another symbol. You will find that these symbols work better and better and are easier to focus on as you meditate each day.

The key to meditation is focus, on the intermediate level. Not just focus, as a vague abstraction, but focus, or focusing, on specific symbols. The symbols are the chakras, an enlightened teacher, enlightened music or light. Now, there are other alternatives. Sometimes you focus on a *yantra* with the eyes open. You know, but then again, it's the same thing. You can't be sitting there focusing on the yantra or colored pebble or whatever it may be, vaguely, vaguely looking at it and allowing your mind to drift. If you're using the visual sight to still the mind, you must focus to the exclusion of everything else.

I like the music better because the music—in particular the meditation albums—is designed to meditate to. If you focus on a yantra, it is a geometric representation of other vortexes of energy, but still, it's a bunch of lines. You know, it's not charged the way the music is. Music is more engulfing. We're dealing with the rhythms, substructures, tonalities. A visual focus is OK, and I recommended it until we had the music. The music is superior, definitely, to the visual focus.

That's why I now recommend that you close your eyes during meditation, if you're using one of the meditation albums. And I've put so much energy into each song, so much bright, brilliant, beautiful energy, and the compositions of course are all based around other dimensions. Each composition references a particular plane of light, that by focusing on the music to the exclusion of everything else, you'll just pull beautiful bright light and go through the music into that light as far as you can. And you'll go a little further each time. Then, when you can't hold on to the music, focus on the teacher in a private way, if you have an enlightened teacher or know one.

It's sort of like the feeling that's between us now. Focus on that energy that's coming through my voice or on any enlightened teacher—be they embodied or disembodied—but not on a bunch of their students or not on one of their students who teaches. Bad mistake. Only on the enlightened. And again, we're not staying with them; we're going through them into the light itself. Or focus on just light. You can imagine light, feel it. Hold it in your mind, though. It can't be vague because then your mind is drifting. It's through substitution that we meditate.

Advanced meditation, which we might talk about another time—it's pretty hard to talk about—is different. It's not substitution. It's transmutation. It's another step, another staging—that's samadhi and the supraconscious. But intermediate meditation will do you, I think, quite well for a while. My recommendation is to know the symbols of your mind and through those symbols to become fully conscious and fully aware, to focus on the chakras while you meditate, to use all three in each meditation. Because you'll be bringing the kundalini up from the root chakra to the crown center. By just focusing on those three, that'll take care of it for you.

Spend a third of your time starting with the navel center, a third of your time on the chest center, a third of your time on the third eye. But during those periods of time, which should be equal, hopefully you'll be listening to enlightened music which will block out the incredible number of vibrations on an overpopulated planet—that you would otherwise be picking up—because you're in a highly psychic state when you meditate. The music will act as an aura block. It will help. It won't do it all. Then you should start each part of the session by focusing on the chakra.

If we're doing the navel center, focus on the chakra as intensely as you can for as long as you can. Then, when the mind tires and you just can't do it, be real about it. Keep a vague feeling of that area throughout that period of that chakra meditation, and now switch to the music. Focus on the music for as long as you can. When you just can't do it, now focus on your teacher. Then focus on light. Then go back to the chakra again. Or in any order. You can mix it up. But for that entire period of that chakra, always have a symbol in your mind that you're focused on. Whenever a person's face, an image, a memory, an anticipation comes in your mind, *fwak* it out. Push it out by returning your mind to the symbol, by returning your mind to light, to the music, to the teacher, a bright moment with the teacher, a pure moment, a beautiful moment of transcendence, or the chakra.

In other words, substitute. Don't just sit there and push the thought out, because then another thought will just come in. Or you'll focus on that thought as you push it out. Instead, move your mind to the symbol. Eventually this gets easier, with practice. Then move to the next chakra when it's time, and the last chakra.

What we're really keying to or looking at is the time you spend sitting there. We're looking more specifically into the moment-to-moment experience while you're focusing on a chakra. It's not enough just to say, "Sit and focus on a chakra." That's introductory meditation. Now we're making sure that it's "quality time," as they say in the 90's.

And keep your sense of humor. Stay funny. And decide if you even want to do any of this. Maybe you don't need to do this. This is a lot of work. It creates ecstasy, liberation and a fine life, sure. But maybe this isn't your moment. Maybe you should just go and do something else. But if you do feel that pull to the eternal, and you can't stay away from it, then it is most important that you meditate properly. Otherwise meditation will do you a disservice. It'll confuse you more than clarify you. It'll bring tremendous impurity in you, if you're allowing your mind to wander during the empowered experience. Keep your mind centered on that which leads to light. Intensively. That's intermediate meditation. Accept no substitutes—and overall, have a nice incarnation.

CHAPTER TWELVE

THE ENLIGHTENMENT CYCLE

Enlightenment is the complete awareness of life without any mental modifications. It is perfect light, light that has always existed, exists now and will always exist. It's the light that exists beyond darkness. It's the core and the center of all things, and it's in all things and beyond all things.

Enlightenment is a state of consciousness, I suppose. It's a way of talking about it. It's something that we attain—if we attain things.

There's a mountain. I'd like to climb to the top of it. There's something very beautiful, very wonderful on top of it—so I hope. I climb up the mountain and when I reach the top, I have a view. If there's something wonderful there, I've found it—if that's what attainment is. The mountain of enlightenment, of course, is inside of us. It's inside of our mind. And we're climbing that mountain every day. Our life is that mountain.

The mountain is complicated. It has a lot of sides, a lot of paths. We can traverse them. We can go up the mountain, down the mountain, around the mountain, forever, and never reach the top. The top is enlightenment—the complete awareness of life without any mental modifications, the highest viewpoint. Not the best, but the highest unobstructed view. And if that's your interest, if you seek enlightenment, then the practice of meditation is the pathway to enlightenment, along with the practice of mindfulness. These are the two things that we do in Buddhism to become enlightened.

Enlightenment exists in everything. Enlightenment is everything. It's around everything, it's through everything and it's beyond everything. It sounds more complicated than it is, actually. If you want to experience enlightenment in a simple way, all you have to do is stop your thoughts. When there is no thought in the mind, no thought of no thought, when the mind is quiet and it rests but is fully alert, we experience a little bit of enlightenment. A little light will filter in.

Our thoughts, our desires, emotions, angers, fears, loves, hates—these are clouds that come between us and the light of the sun. When those things stop, when thought goes away, and fear and anxiety, alienation, depression, even hope—even hope—then when these things clear away, there's light, perfect light, an all-encompassing light. That's a word that I use for it. I don't know of a better word in English. Maybe we could say an ecstatic light, a light that is encompassing of all things—God, knowledge, purity, truth. But light is good enough for me. I think it suffices.

Enlightenment exists within you. And as I said, there's this mountain that we're climbing every day. How's your climb going? It's uphill. If you're going towards enlightenment, and if it seems like it's very easy and it's downhill, then you're probably going towards enlightenment, too.

Awareness is infinite. And I want you to understand that enlightenment is not something that is attained or reached by a select few. I mean, obviously it is attained or reached by a select few, in that very few people seem to attain it or reach it. But that's not because it's incredibly hard. It's just not incredibly popular.

What's so hard about being happy? What's so hard about giving up fear, giving up hate, giving up anxiety? It would seem to me that these are very sensible things to do—to be happy forever, to see beyond this cosmic dream that we call life and see other dreams of the cosmos, dimensions of mind, of time, space and things beyond that.

To go to the very center of the mind of God, to be that, to become aware of our infiniteness, is the goal of Buddhism—one of the goals. Along the way, to be as kind to others as possible without thinking that we're particularly wonderful because we are, perhaps, kind. To transcend our identity, in other words, to go beyond ego, to become conscious of life in constantly new ways, as is life conscious of itself in constantly new ways.

To get through all this rhetoric, let's say that the process of becoming enlightenment itself is simply a process of getting out of the way—if enlightenment is there, if it exists, which of course it does. Take my word for it. It's something incredible, better than you can possibly imagine, fabulous beyond comprehension, ecstatic beyond wonder, beautiful beyond seeing and understanding. And if it's already there inside us and all things, all we have to do is get something out of the way that's causing us not to see and experience that—and that's *us*. It sounds silly, but it's true.

Our limited way of perceiving things, of perceiving life; the way that we think of ourselves, think of others, think of the world; the karmic patterns that we've evolved in all these countless lifetimes we've passed through and in this life; the very way that we collate information, process it and experience it; the information of life, of living, perception—the study of enlightenment, that is to say, that which we go through to become enlightened, is really a reorganization of our perceptual body or our perceptual field. We learn to see life more directly and more clearly.

You're driving a car. You're trying to see where you're going, but if the windshield is really dirty, it's hard. If it's completely opaque, you can't see at all. We need to have a clear windshield to see where we're going. The light is already there. It's all-present. It's perfect. It's enlightenment. But something is obscuring the window, the view, the mirror of self-reflection.

As they say sometimes in Zen Buddhism, there's a little speck of dust on the mirror, and that's us—our personality, our view, our loves, our hates, our desires, our self-importance, our self-pity—ourselves. Or perhaps a deeper self is that light that's on the other side of this being we conceive of ourselves to be, what we experience.

In Buddhism, we meditate. We make our mind quiet by learning to focus on the chakras, release internal energy that we call kundalini, and bring ourselves into clear and high states of consciousness. We go up on top of the mountain or as high as we can get. When we're on top of the mountain, we look around and we gain a new view of things. Then we come down a little bit and we lead our daily lives. But we don't quite come down as far as we were before. And then we climb up a little higher in our next meditation and then we come down again, not quite as far as before. Gradually we go up to the top of the mountain of enlightenment.

Well, there isn't really a top. It's sort of like the Himalayas. Once you get way up to the top of one, you see that there are a lot more mountains up top, and there are more ranges to climb, and they seem to go on forever, as far as the horizon, and that's good enough for me.

Enlightenment is endless. There's no end to it. There's no beginning to it. It's perfect. It goes on forever. It's part of you. It's part of me. It's part of everything. And that perception, if it gives you joy, is there for you to have—if you learn to meditate, if you practice mindfulness, which is simply learning to be in very happy and positive states of mind when you're not actually sitting and meditating—it's a kind of a moving meditation. When your life becomes clear and pure, like clear and pure water, like the snow in the Himalayas, like the wind, when your mind is clear and your view of life is unobstructed, then you'll be at peace with yourself. You'll be happy.

Enlightenment is not just again, a little burst of light. It means that your mind has become one with the universe, with all things. And it's not as if you think of a lot of things simultaneously because you'd be thinking, wouldn't you? It's not as if you'd be reflecting on some deep inner truth or having a conversation with God or Goddess or something like that. Not really. I mean, you can do that, I guess. But true enlightenment is beyond words to express.

I'm just suggesting, as others have, that there's something perfect on the other side of pain and limitation and frustration, and that's life—in an unmodified form. It's what we come out of; it's what we return to. And you don't have to be in so much pain if you meditate. As a matter of fact, you can experience ecstasy.

Life still hurts at times—hurts to have a body at times, hurts to be born, hurts to live, hurts to die. But it can also be ecstasy beyond comprehension. And people who practice meditation correctly—who follow the pathway to enlightenment, who learn to love and not hate, who learn to control themselves and go beyond personality to something more perfect—know that ecstasy. You can know that ecstasy. It's inside of you. It's inside all things. It's everywhere and nowhere. It's one of those Buddhist riddles. We like riddles in Buddhism.

As an enlightened teacher of Buddhism, I'd like to welcome you to the pathway to enlightenment. I'd like to encourage you, based upon my own personal experience and the personal experience of countless others, to meditate—to be more positive, to engage in the practice of meditation, to learn how to do this wonderful thing, to make your mind still in a crazy world, where everybody's at war with everybody and certainly with ourselves. I'd like you to learn to be happy and to see things more brightly.

You don't have to. You can be miserable, if it's your prerogative. You can make others suffer, if it's your prerogative, and that'll cause you to suffer more. Or you can say, "Wait a minute," you know, "Hold on. Press the pause button." Let's think about this or not think about it, as the case may be. You're just going to die and be reborn and die and be reborn forever. And just as changing to a new city doesn't necessarily change your life that much—because all cities are really about the same, because wherever you go there you are—changing incarnations doesn't change that much.

What's the rush? What changes something is identity. When we change our identity, when we expand our view of ourselves, when we recode the way the structures of our mind work, that's what Buddhism really is—it's a redefinition. We rework the mind. We believe that the mind is not something that's solid. It's like water. It's fluid. When you place water in a container, it takes a shape. If I place it in a round glass, it'll be round, in a rectangular glass, it'll be rectangular. We feel that the mind is like water and it takes whatever shape we put it in, and its current shape is our personality, our view of the world, which has grown about from our experiences in this and past lives. If we change its shape, then the mind will change shape. If we change the view we have of existence, then everything changes.

And meditation and mindfulness, just those two simple things, will do that, gradually, a little at a time—maybe not so gradually, maybe sometimes in leaps and bounds. It varies from day to day. It depends on how deeply you meditate, how intensely you practice mindfulness, how happy you want to be. And it's entirely up to you. That's the beauty of life, in my opinion. We can't necessarily always help what happens to us. We're born into poverty, we're born into wealth, we're born into something in the middle. But we can do something about our condition.

Sometimes we can't even do anything about our social condition, but we can do something about our condition, our condition of light. We can meditate and practice mindfulness. We can do it in a mansion, we can do it in a jail cell, we can do it in mediocrity. It really doesn't matter. What matters is that we gain control of our mind. We can't always control the circumstances of our lives. We try as best we can. But what we can do is gain control of our mind and direct it towards that all-perfect light within ourselves.

Now, becoming enlightened doesn't mean everything works out your way. I mean, some people have dime-store definitions of enlightenment, and they think, "Oh, well, if I become enlightened that means I'll get everything I want." Untrue. It means you won't want anything. It means that you will be happy, and if things go your way, you're happy, and if things don't, you're happy. That doesn't mean you're a moron who doesn't care. It means you're in a state of understanding, you have the depth where you see yourself in an incarnate body going through time and space in the lifetime, and at the same time, you're beyond all this—not spaced out, rather conscious.

It makes the colors more vivid, the moments of life more important, and at the same time, the immediacy of the pain is not as important, really, because we see eternity. The transient arises and falls. All things end. New things begin. And we have the perspective of eternity to view that from, and so when things don't work out, we can accept that joyfully, quietly, sometimes with laughter.

When things don't work out, we can accept it. When they do, we can celebrate that too. Because our happiness is not dependent upon what occurs to us every day, physically, in the world, or the changes our physical body undergoes. Our happiness comes from within, our experience of endless stages of consciousness, of ecstasy, of bliss, of brightness, of beauty, of love—things that are within us. If we meditate, we become conscious of these things. We climb the mountain a little higher. We see life a little more truly perhaps. We clear the window a little bit better so we can see where we're going, and maybe sometimes that makes things more beautiful—certainly more accurate.

I would encourage you to become enlightened, to follow the pathway to enlightenment, to learn to meditate, to practice mindfulness; and not to really care what anybody thinks about you, including yourself, unless it's very positive.

You know, I've been teaching meditation and Buddhism for many, many lifetimes, and in this lifetime, for many, many years. And I've learned a few things—I don't think a lot of things, but a few things. One of the things that I've learned is that most people don't care much about enlightenment and the truth. You know, they'd rather watch the Home Shopping Network, and maybe that's another kind of enlightenment and truth. But you might, and it really doesn't matter if anybody else cares. If you're the only person who cares in the world, then that matters the world for you, and you should find yourself a teacher of enlightenment.

True teachers of enlightenment are hard to find. The popular ones, of course, usually aren't enlightened because how could they be? They just tell people what they want to hear. The unpopular ones usually are because they tell you the truth, and who wants to hear that? Not the people who watch the Home Shopping Network, no offense to the Home Shopping Network intended, because in the world of interactive, multi-media highways, we're all traveling somewhere interactively and we're all shopping for something. And what are we shopping for? Our dreams, our hopes, our ambitions for ourselves, for those we love, the demise of those we don't care about, you know, these little scenarios we play out endlessly in our mind—it just doesn't matter. I mean it does, of course, at one moment, and then we look somewhere else like a child does after they've been crying and they lost their toy, and suddenly they've forgotten and they're happy in a new moment. Well, that's life.

But consistency is nice, I think, personally. I like to be consistently happy. I like to be consistently more aware and more conscious of the truth. That's just my particular bent. And what I like about Buddhism and meditation and being enlightened, which is an endless process, by the way, is that it gives me that consistency. It's not somebody's belief that they want to force upon me for their reasons or for their fears—they had to believe in this—or their fantasies. I don't really care about all that. I just want to know.

I want to know what are the limits, if there are any. What can I do with this thing called life? Why is everybody so unhappy? Are there other options? If there are, I want to exercise them, and I do. Which is why I began the study so many lifetimes ago, and I teach meditation and the pathway to enlightenment because I know that there are other people who—like I did a long time ago and continue to do today, of course—want to climb that mountain to the highest light. And since there were others a long time ago who were kind enough to give me a hard time and allow me to study with them, I try and express the same Buddhist courtesy by teaching others a little bit about the short path to enlightenment, Tantric Buddhism. So, meditation and mindfulness. These are the things that we are interested in—how to go beyond pain, fear and limitation, how to experience that brightness.

Well, a few hints. Begin by meditating. Meditation means that each day you sit for a period of time and you don't move your body. Sit nice and still. Sit up straight. You practice a meditation technique, at least to start with. This usually involves focusing on something, taking your mind and focusing on a chakra, an energy center in your body, or sometimes something external, visually, with your eyes open. Some people use mantras—words they repeat in their mind or out loud. Some people do visualizations, where they hold an image in their mind. Some focus on their breathing. There are lots of ways to do it, but the effect is the same. It makes the mind quiet. I personally recommend meditating on the chakras. That's the short path method.

You sit for 15 minutes—maybe in the beginning, after a while, half an hour, 45 minutes, an hour—and you focus, as a teacher of meditation will instruct you. And if you can do it once a day, that's great. If you can do it twice, that's fabulous.

Read books that inspire you about meditation, Buddhism, Hinduism, Taoism, any "ism" you want. If they're clear, they should all say the same thing. They should direct you towards that which is the highest and the brightest and the most beautiful—enlightenment. And whatever inspires you to do that morning meditation or evening meditation, or to practice mindfulness during the day, is good. I don't care what it's called, who wrote it, whether they're popular or unpopular, known or unknown. If it works for you, that's good—if it gets you to meditate.

Now, reading books about enlightenment does not make you

enlightened at all. You can read all the books about all the lives of the Buddhas and everyone's wonderful perceptions, and that won't make you enlightened. You have to meditate yourself. You can read about weight lifting or track or swimming; that reading won't produce the effect. It'll take you on a mental journey perhaps. It might get you to start, but Buddha's point is true. In order to become enlightened, you need to meditate. And it's fun. It's really not hard. I mean, I suppose it's hard, but isn't it harder to be unhappy and in pain than to be happy and in ecstasy?

Self-knowledge, I guess, is hard. But I think pain is harder, personally. I think to be hopeless is very hard. I think to die without hope or to live without hope is very hard. To just burn out, to give up just because things don't go your way, to assume that there's no God, no infinite light, I mean, I think that's pretty petty, personally. I've felt that way at times. I think we all have. We get frustrated. But when you meditate each day, you go beyond that. You get renewed. All this wonderful energy unlocks inside you, from deep within you, and flows through your body and mind and renews you. It gives you the ability to fight again, to believe again, to love again and to climb the mountain a little bit higher, to get a new view.

That's what really renews us, isn't it? When we just suddenly break through those barriers, those limitations, when we do something we've never done that's wonderful. Then energy floods us and our consciousness is lifted. And that's what meditation is, and if meditation is not doing that for you—if you practice—now, you're not meditating. You're sitting, thinking, spacing out and wasting your time. When you walk away from a meditation session, you should feel better. You should feel more optimistic. You should be brighter.

In the beginning, you won't be completely consistent, it's true. You're learning a new art. The first day you start to study a language, you can't speak it. But you might learn one word, and that's a start. And it's fun to learn a new language, and it's fun to learn to meditate, and it's fun to feel better and to be hopeful and to be wiser than we've been before.

Meditation doesn't work if you don't do it. The main thing is to meditate. And at first you may be sporadic. You'll just get up and meditate once in a while. But if you like it, you'll come back to it and it will become a regular practice—and if you don't, well, it's not your time yet.

Mindfulness is a little different. It simply means that as we go through the day, at least initially, we learn to gain control of our mind, our emotions. When we could get angry, we don't because anger burns up a lot of energy, and we feel tired and exhausted and it doesn't make other people feel any better. We learn to conserve energy in a variety of simple and complicated ways that we learn in Buddhist practice so that throughout the day, we're in a nicer state of mind. We feel happy. We're just, you know, we're not totally burned out at the end of the day. And if we are, we sit down and meditate, and we climb the mountain a little higher, and all that washes away, and we feel better than perhaps we felt all day, and even in our morning meditation.

Life is a circle, you know—that's what we believe as Buddhists—or a series of circles that are all existing simultaneously, and we move around the circle for a while, and if we know how, if we're skillful in meditation, we can get into another circle and move around that. We move around these silly circles forever throughout eternity, and we're all those circles, and there is emptiness within them and beyond them. And right now we're somewhere in the circumference of the circle—looking across, looking behind us, having just passed through something, going towards something.

Enlightenment is a circle, different circle. Meditation brings us to that circle. Eventually, it brings us to the center of it. Eventually, we become enlightenment itself, somewhere down the line.

Meditation is a bright, hopeful practice in which we learn to make our mind quiet so that the infinite, perfect light of enlightenment can flow through us. It awakens us to life. And we can have lived many years and many lifetimes and think we've seen it all, and what a foolish thought because we can't have seen it all—we can hardly have seen any of it since it goes on forever. Life that is; enlightenment is endless.

There's something new at every moment, in every moment. But if we're in the same state of mind, well then, we just self-reflect. We just see our self in that moment, and things are dull and kind of gray and kind of boring, which means that we're not very awakened, are we? On the other hand, if at every moment the world is bright and shining—which it truly is, by the way—then we're in a steady stream of light. We're on the pathway to enlightenment.

Meditation and the practice of mindfulness over a period of time will help you to live in the states of brightness. Having a good teacher is very important because the practice is quite complicated, as it gets—as you get further along—it becomes very sophisticated. A good teacher will empower you, yell at you, not tell you what you want to hear, tell you the truth about how to meditate, how to get your act together, how to get organized, how to develop yourself fully, how to control yourself, how to have a more positive image and then move beyond that image to perfection. Good teachers are not known for telling you what you want to hear, and consequently they're rarely popular because they tend to offend people on a regular basis by their mere presence on earth, it seems.

Because people don't really want to know the truth. The truth is that you're all dead in the future, everything that you do has no point, and all of the achievements of the human race are meaningless. That's the truth. If you don't think so, go visit Egypt sometime or ancient Greece, and look at all those wonderful edifices that are just burned-out stone now. Museumware. And yet, and yet, and yet, enlightenment is part of that. Ah, we're back to Buddhist mysteries, Buddhist fun. Enlightenment is part of it.

Those moments were beautiful, I guess, when they were doing all that. But they pass. They're transient. And none of this matters a bit. Yet, of course it matters at that moment. We try and be mindful of the moment, this moment in incarnation, in awareness, where we're alive and experiencing whatever life is putting before us and putting us in and through. And we try to be bright and positive and understand it, but it's fleeting.

Nothing lasts. Youth fades. Flowers fade. Passion fades. But life itself goes on forever. And when you know that, you figure, "Well I might as well learn how to deal with this life thing since it's gonna go on forever; since I live forever in one lifetime or another in one body or another, I might as well learn to do it right because it will be better for me." I mean, I think that's an intelligent way for you to look at things. And so meditation is something that, when you learn to do it in this life, of course, that knowledge will accompany you to your next life and so on and so forth.

What you gain in internal knowledge goes from one lifetime to another. It's not wasted. Unlike those stone edifices that will fade, your internal knowledge will stay with you from one incarnation to another. It comes back; it's like an inheritance.

You remember. You're drawn back to the pathway to enlightenment, to meditation, and when you begin to meditate your past life knowledge returns to you. Your achievements, if that's what we want to call them, that place you got to on the mountain before, you gradually work your way back up to it, or rapidly. Then you continue from there and go forward into the world of light and enlightenment and brightness—beyond pain, beyond frustration, beyond illusion—there's perfect light, an all-perfect light that no one has a monopoly on.

But meditation is the pathway to enlightenment, and I would encourage you to follow that pathway as far as you can, into ecstasy.

Made in United States
North Haven, CT
28 May 2024

53039678R00137